PLAYING FOR COACH MEYER

Steve Smiley
Northern State University
Player from 1999-2004

Note for Librarians: A cataloguing record for this book is available from Library and Archives
Canada at www.collectionscanada.ca/amicus/index-e.html
ISBN 1-4120-7250-6

*Printed in Victoria, BC, Canada. Printed on paper with minimum 30% recycled fibre. Trafford's print shop
runs on "green energy" from solar, wind and other environmentally-friendly power sources.*

PUBLISHING™
Offices in Canada, USA, Ireland and UK
This book was published *on-demand* in cooperation with Trafford Publishing. On-demand
publishing is a unique process and service of making a book available for retail sale to the
public taking advantage of on-demand manufacturing and Internet marketing. On-demand
publishing includes promotions, retail sales, manufacturing, order fulfilment, accounting and
collecting royalties on behalf of the author.

Book sales for North America and international:
Trafford Publishing, 6E–2333 Government St.,
Victoria, BC v8t 4p4 CANADA
phone 250 383 6864 (toll-free 1 888 232 4444)
fax 250 383 6804; email to orders@trafford.com
Book sales in Europe:
Trafford Publishing (uk) Limited, 9 Park End Street, 2nd Floor
Oxford, UK ox1 1hh UNITED KINGDOM
phone 44 (0)1865 722 113 (local rate 0845 230 9601)
facsimile 44 (0)1865 722 868; info.uk@trafford.com
Order online at:
trafford.com/05-2145

10 9 8 7 6 5 4 3 2

Dedicated to My Beautiful Wife, Nikki;
My Mom, Claudia; My Dad, Tim; My Brother, Matt;
All of My Teammates, Coaches, and Friends in Aberdeen;
And of Course, to Coach Meyer Himself,
My Inspiration for Writing This Story

CONTENTS

ACKNOWLEDGEMENTS

To the 25 players, coaches, and administrators that helped to share a story about Coach Meyer.

To Sundance Wicks, who was a huge part in helping contact former Lipscomb players, editing the manuscript, and writing an inspiring foreword to the story.

To my mom, Claudia Smiley, for finding old pictures of my playing days that were included in this story.

To my wife, Nikki, for helping with the editing process.

To Rob Browne, Greg Glenn, Jason Shelton, Greg Eubanks, Barbara Anderson, and all of the other Lipscomb players for helping to contact their former teammates.

For Nick Kornder, and the rest of the Sports Information Office at Northern State University, for allowing me to use some of their pictures in the story, including the cover picture.

And for everybody else that I may have forgotten; I am grateful to all of you.

Generosity...

While there were so many people that contributed and donated to this story in so many different ways, I want to give a special thanks to each and every person that contributed a financial donation to make this project a reality. I want to especially thank all of the former Lipscomb players, most of whom have never met me, yet still believed in this project and contributed. I especially thank Rob Browne, who relentlessly chased after his old teammates and found a way to help round out the necessary funds. Thank you all.

Playing for Coach Meyer Donation List (as of September 17th, 2005)

- Rob Browne
- Richard Taylor
- Brian Ayers
- Andy Blackston
- Greg Glenn
- Phil Hutcheson
- Mark Campbell
- Marcus Bodie
- Wade Tomlinson
- Bob Olson
- Tony Birmingham
- Brian Zehnder
- Dustin Hjelmeland
- Barbara Anderson
- Jarod Obering

FOREWORD
IF YOU ARE JUST A COACH...

Coach Meyer once told me that if he were to write a book he would title it, "If You Are Just a Coach." The funny thing is that one split second was the only time I had ever heard him talk about a book being written about him; he had never mentioned it before, nor has he mentioned it since. Coach says a lot of things, but for some reason that stood out in my mind. It stood out because it was the only time in my entire five years with him that I had ever heard him mention a single word about himself. Coach Meyer embodies servant leadership. Any program he has ever been associated with, he has devoted his life to it and he would be the first one to tell you that he is receiving far more than he is giving.

By the end of my time at Northern State University with Coach Meyer I developed the habit of analyzing every single thing that he would say. First I would write it down, and then I would analyze it. I'm not a gambler, but I am willing to put money on it that I am not the only player he has coached that developed the syndrome of over-analysis. When I started to analyze the title, "If You Are Just a Coach," it all began to make sense to me. Some coaches are excellent golfers, others are avid hunters, and I know a lot of coaches who can put a worm on a hook a lot better than Coach Meyer probably could. But if you are a just a coach, that is all you are. If you are just a coach, the team is all you have and they consume your thoughts. If you are just a coach, you cherish every moment with the team and never take a teachable moment for granted. If you are just a coach, you can't get your natural high by golfing, hunting or fishing. If you are just a coach, your example isn't the main thing, it is the only thing. If you are just a coach, the journey of building a team is always greater than the destination. If you are just a coach, you are easy to please but very hard to satisfy. If you are just a coach that is all you are. If you are just a coach, and coaching is what you love, then you are blessed; and if you are blessed in your work, you need no other blessing.

In this day and age it is hard to find somebody who wants to be who they are. Everybody always wants to be someone else or be somewhere else, but sometimes the place where you are is where you were meant to be. Coach Meyer is just a coach. He probably never golfed and couldn't if he tried, but he can do one thing better than anybody I have ever seen, and that is teach the game of basketball and how it relates to life. For two years he was needed to impact the lives of young men at Hamline University. For twenty four years he was needed to impact the lives of the young men at David Lipscomb University in Nashville, Tennessee. And for the last six years he was needed to impact the lives of the young men at Northern State University in Aberdeen, South Dakota. I just happened to be one of many in the long line of changed lives. I have received a blessing from the Lord up above, and I like to call that blessing by his name, Coach Meyer. Thanks for being a friend, an inspiration and my coach.

Pride in the Pack,
Sundance M. Wicks

BECOMING REAL

Steve Smiley tells an intriguing story of developing into an outstanding young person. This is a **REAL** tale of the highs and lows, the experiences that helped mold him through his **TEAM** experience in college basketball.

It reveals the depth of human relationships that can be gained from the life lessons gained from the challenges of sports with the critical leadership of a caring, passionate coach who forges shared ownership in his basketball teams.

Don Meyer is just such a coach who assists / challenges Steve Smiley and other Northern players into being a **TEAM** and becoming / developing into **REAL** people.

As a player I was privileged to Coach, Don was always interested in developing the best **TEAM**. He continues to focus on the quest to "play against the game," as well as becoming the best he can be. I highly recommend this journey of college basketball at it's best – a life-changing experience.

Jerry Krause
Gonzaga University

"AN INTRODUCTION"

Throughout my 5 years at Northern, I always wanted to do something after my playing days were over to somehow show Coach Meyer my appreciation for what he had done for me. It took me almost the duration of my career to finally decide what that would be, but throughout my entire time at Northern I always wrote down in a type of journal the experiences and thoughts that I had. I think it was at the end of my junior year that I finally came upon the idea of writing a book about Coach Meyer and about my playing days for the Wolves. I always had the feeling that Coach Meyer didn't get as much respect on a local or national level as he deserved. While he was extremely well-known in the world of high school, college, and even professional coaches, and even though coaches used his instructional videos at all levels, I continually had the feeling that people didn't appreciate Coach Meyer in the way that other legendary coaches, such as John Wooden, Bob Knight, Mike Krzyzewski and Pat Summit were appreciated. This no doubt stemmed from the fact that Coach Meyer never coached at the Division 1 level or in the pros, but his accomplishments as a coach and, more importantly, his impact as a teacher, should still be shared with all who wanted to listen.

By the time I finished my playing days and began writing this story in the spring of 2004, Coach Meyer had already reached the number eight spot in all-time wins in college basketball (regardless of level, including all NCAA divisions and all NAIA divisions) with 793 career wins in 32 years of coaching (an average of 25 wins per year), surpassing legends Jerry Tarkanian, Henry Iba, and Phog Allen, to name a few. In 1986, he won the NAIA national championship at David Lipscomb University and his 1989 team set a college basketball record with 41 wins. He helped mold players that came to be the first and second all-time leading scorers in college basketball history in John Pierce and Philip Hutcheson, respectively. He also coached his son, Jerry, who became the record holder in college basketball for assists in a career. In addition, he continued to touch the lives of countless individuals in the basketball world through his instructional videos, summer coaching academies, free-fall clinics, and countless hours of teaching the game to whoever would listen.

Above all else, Coach Meyer was a teacher. He wanted to teach the game to any and everyone, from the first-grade campers to college athletes, who would come to Coach for advice on all aspects of the game. Coach was obsessed about the fundamentals of the game, down to the very smallest details, and because of this obsession, it was very difficult at times to play for Coach Meyer. He always demanded perfection, realizing that we would not be able to ever obtain it, but always pushing us to search for it in everything that we did. And to Coach Meyer, perfection did not stop once we left the basketball floor. Coach demanded perfection in all parts of our lives. If you weren't getting the job done in class or socially, you were going to hear about it, and if you didn't get the message on your own, Coach had no problem "reinforcing" the message in a variety of different manners. In demanding perfection from us in everything we did, Coach made us reach for higher ground and he made us try to be the best people that we possibly could be. To me, that is what made Coach Meyer a little different. As players, we could all tell how much Coach cared for us, and I believe that is why we played so hard for him. There was no way that we could let him down by not caring as much as he did. There was always a respect between the coaches and the players in our program and although everybody had to sacrifice for the team, it was a sacrifice that the true players willingly made to be a part of something special.

My goal in writing this story was to show people what the life of a college basketball player (that had the privilege to play for Coach Meyer) was all about. I knew that my story alone was only a very small piece of the bigger picture, and so after finishing the story, I tried to reach out to as many former players, coaches and administrators that had worked with Coach Meyer as possible, in hopes that they would also share pieces of their stories. At the end of each of the first four "years" of this book, there is a section entitled *In Their Words*, and I firmly believe that these stories from other people are what really paint the true picture of Coach Meyer from so many different angles. I am truly grateful to everybody that took the time to share some of their own stories to make this story of Coach Meyer so much more complete. I couldn't have pulled this off without each one of you. Finally, while there is no way for me to fully describe and show what type of man Coach Meyer truly is in these few short pages, I hope that this story will help people understand what a Coach Meyer program is all about and finally appreciate him for the legend that he is. I hope you enjoy.

Steve Smiley

A QUICK BACKGROUND:

Northern State University is a small, NCAA Division II school located in Aberdeen, South Dakota. Around 3,000 people attend the university and the entire city (which is the third largest city in the state) only has a population of around 30,000. It is the classic Midwestern town, where people still have good morals and values and rarely get caught up in the stresses that can be found in bigger cities. Coach Meyer always joked that when he would drive into Aberdeen he would know that he was approaching when he saw a sign on the road that said, "Welcome to Aberdeen: Turn back your clocks twenty years." The truth is that he was absolutely right. Aberdeen is a place that is quiet and simple, and it provided in absolutely great setting for a college student.

Because there isn't much to do in Aberdeen socially, the people in the area absolutely are crazy about the local sports scene, including Northern State University and the high school sports in the area. In the winter time, the temperature regularly drops well below 0 degrees, so all of the activities are indoors, and people come from all over the surrounding areas to see the NSU Wolves play. When I was at Northern, every year we ranked in the top five in attendance for NCAA Division II, usually averaging somewhere around 3,000 fans per game. Our home floor, Wachs Arena, was always jammed on game night, and when we played games against rival teams in our conference or from around the state, the arena would sometimes fill to 6,000 people or more. It was absolutely an amazing environment to play in, and I have never been around a place like Aberdeen since I left, where people are so crazy about basketball. There are so many good basketball programs throughout the country that just don't have much of a fan base, either because the school is in a big city where there are just too many other things for people to do, or just because people don't care. I never knew how grateful I would be to play in an atmosphere like the one at Northern, and I also never realized when I was there how much I would miss it once I left. If you ever get a chance to come to the Midwest, or if you ever want to be a part of an amazing atmosphere, just look on the map for a town in the northeast corner of South Dakota named Aberdeen, and you can find it right there.

Wachs Arena: A Special Place

O‌DE TO A **CHAMPION**

HE IS DRY YET SLY, OBVIOUS AND STEALTH, OPEN
YET INWARD, GIVING BUT FRUGAL, SERVING AND
DEMANDING, POOR AND WEALTHY, A CONFIDANT
AND CONFIDER, LEADER OF BISONS AND SLAVE
TO COACHES (ESPECIALLY HIS OWN), THE BUSIEST
MAN I KNOW YET THE ONE WITH THE MOST TIME
IF WE NEED IT, BRILLIANT, ENERGETIC, FANATICAL,
DISCIPLINED, FUNNY, OBSESSED, STRANGE, BALD
,SOMETIMES FAT AND SOMETIMES SKINNY, A GREAT
LAUGHER AND A LOUD BARKER, THE MASTER CLINI-
CIAN.
HE WAS BASE AND BALD AND DROVE A CHEVETTE
STRANGE AND QUIET AND SEEMED ALWAYS TO FRET
"DO YOU WANT TO BE A BISON" IN A GROWLY VOICE
"IF BASKETBALLS NOT YOUR LIFE, LIPSCOMB ISN'T
YOUR CHOICE
YOU WILL PLAY HARD AND SMART AND NOTHING
FANCY TO SHOW
NO LOAFING, DRIBBLING, HIGH FIVING OR EVEN
SHOOTING OR YOU'LL HAVE TO GO"
SOUNDS GREAT SO WHEN DO WE START?
"THE DAY OF YOUR HIGH SCHOOL GRADUATION
FROM CIVILIZATION YOU'LL DEPART"
WHY, I DON'T KNOW WE CHOSE THIS MAN
RANTING AND RAVING AND DEMANDING HIS PLAN

9

BUT AREN'T WE ALL BETTER BECAUSE OF THIS NUT
THREATENING OUR MAMAS AND DADS AND EVEN
OUR BUTTS
HE MADE US BELIEVE THAT WE WERE QUITE GOOD
THAT TEAMWORK, SERVICE AND HARD WORK
WOULD
ALLOW US SOME WINS AND MUCH MUCH MORE
DEVELOPING CHAMPIONS REGARDLESS THE SCORE
SO NOW WE RETURN TO HONOR THE MAN
WHO HAS GIVEN HIS LIFE TO HIS ALL IMPORTANT
PLAN
THAT GIVING ONE'S BEST IS BY GOD REQUIRED
AND ANYTHING LESS IS NOT PART OF COACH
MEYER
THANK YOU COACH FOR THIS LESSON ON LIFE
YOU ARE A HUGE PART OF ME, MY CHILDREN, AND
WIFE
CARRY ON WITH THE MISSION THOUGH DETRAC-
TORS ABOUND
WE ARE ALL MUCH BETTER BECAUSE YOU ARE
AROUND
YOU'VE IMPROVED YOUR DRESS NO MORE DOUBLE
KNITS
NO POLYESTER, BELL BOTTOMS OR EVEN WINGTIPS
YOU DRIVE A NICE CAR AND YOUR HOUSE IS A
HAVEN
AND HEAVEN ONLY KNOWS WHY CAPTAIN D"S
YOU'RE STILL CRAVEN
YOU SEEMED TO HAVE MELLOWED IN ALL YOUR
OLD AGE
YOU MIGHT WANT TO CHANGE BACK TO THAT
NASTY UNPREDICTABLE SAGE
FOR BACK WHEN SUICIDES WERE RUN EVERY DAY
WE KICKED BELMONT'S BUTT IN EVERY WAY

DO YOU REMEMBER DRIVING US UNTIL WE WERE
SICK
AND THEN FROM BEHIND GIVING US A KICK
CAMPS ARE BIGGER NOW AND LAWYERS ADVISE
YOUR OLD WAYS WERE BARBARIC AND NOT VERY
WISE
BUT MIGHT WE REMIND YOU THAT PRIDE'S ON THE
LINE
HEY, DO WHAT IT TAKES TO BEAT ALL OF THOSE
SWINE
MONEY AND IMAGE AND CORRECTNESS AND SUCH
BEAT AND BEAT UM BAD; INSTILL CHUCK'S
FAVORITE TOUCH
SO FOR ALL OF US THAT HAVE GONE ON BEFORE
KEEP PRESSING AND DRIVING REGARDLESS THE
SCORE
PRESSURE THE BALL AND GET IN THEIR FACE
INCREASE THE TEMPO, INTENSIFY THE PACE
IT'S THE BISON WAY TO ALWAYS ATTACK
GET EVERY LOOSE BALL AND START ALL WITH A
STACK
DON'T CHANGE IT AT ALL JUST KEEP ON REFINING
HOLDING THE EDGE AND MASTERING TIMING
GOOD LUCK IN 96 IT IS THE YEAR FOR A RING
A DECADE IS LONG ENOUGH WITHOUT A CHAMPI-
ONSHIP FLING

By Ricky Bowers, Former Player, David Lipscomb University

11

1999 - 2000:
"THE BEGINNING OF THE JOURNEY"
REDSHIRT YEAR

Being Recruited...

When I was playing my high school ball in Denver, I always dreamed of playing at a big-time Division I school. While I didn't know where I would actually end up, I was at a level where I was getting recruited by both the mid and lower-level Division I schools and many Division II schools. I had never heard of Northern State University but I remember exactly when their interest in me began. I was playing at a team camp the July following my junior year of high school at the University of Wyoming, and one of Northern's assistant coaches, Paul Sather, was at the Wyoming camp looking for possible recruits. At the time, Wyoming was showing mild interest in me, and it was a place that I would have really considered, so when Coach Sather approached my dad (who was the head coach of our high school team) about what I was looking to do in the future, I wasn't extremely interested. I had never even been to South Dakota, and I still had my heart set on being a Division I player. However, the seed had been planted in my head, and as I began to receive letters from NSU, I started to see not only how successful the program had been, but also how much interest they had in me.

While I maybe received a letter from a D.I school every

two or three weeks, I always received letters from Northern that kept me up to date on their program and I liked how diligent and consistent they were throughout the entire recruiting process. Right before my senior season started, Coach Sather and Coach Olson (who was the head coach at the time) flew my dad and me to Aberdeen for an official visit (my dad had to pay his own way). I still really didn't know what to expect but I was excited to go on my first college visit. The weekend that we went was actually Thanksgiving weekend, so I wasn't able to get a feel for the college atmosphere, but the team had a holiday tournament at the time, and I was able to see a game and then spend a lot of time with the players. By the time my dad and I flew back home on Sunday morning, I knew that Coach Olson and the entire NSU program were serious about having a team atmosphere, winning games, and more importantly, presenting themselves in a quality matter.

As I went through my senior season I still hoped that I would get an offer from a Division I school, but I also knew that if that didn't happen, Northern State was the place that I wanted to be. About two weeks after my season ended, I still hadn't received any firm offers from any Division I schools, and by that time I was already hoping that indeed Northern was the place that I was going to play. The Wolves were fresh off another league championship, 20-win season, and national tournament appearance and I wanted to be a part of a successful program. I remember Coach Olson calling me and offering me a scholarship, and that was it. I was set. I couldn't wait to get to school in the fall and start my NSU career.

The Summer before School...

The only other recruit that Northern had signed for the upcoming year was a 6'5" forward from Gillette, Wyoming named Sundance Wicks. Naturally, Sunny and I were going to be paired as roommates for the following year, so we eventually got in touch with each other to see what we had to bring to school. Just by talking on the phone, we quickly saw that we had a lot in common and we were both excited to get to school to start working out. We talked a few times during that summer, but we never actually met until the first day of school in the fall.

Nothing really eventful happened during that summer until somewhere around the 1st of August. I remember Coach Olson calling me to tell me he had some news. Now, what I didn't mention before was that Coach Olson was the main reason that I chose Northern. He had a personality and an integrity about him that convinced me he was serious about not only winning games and putting banners in the arena, but also about molding his players into quality people. Anyways, Coach Olson called me and told me that he was no longer going to be the coach at Northern. Instead, he was going to take the Athletic Director job that had been offered to him at the school. I was extremely disappointed to say the least. I had no control over who the new coach was going to be and I was worried about a lot of things, including if the new coach was going to bring in a whole new staff or bring in players of his own. Many times in college basketball it happens where a new coach comes to a program, bringing his own staff, and recruiting new players to fit his or her style of play, and the players already at the program end up in a sticky situation. Luckily, when the new coach was announced, it was revealed that the entire staff would be staying, which brought me some peace.

When Coach Olson called and told me who the new head coach was, I had never heard of Don Meyer. Before I had ever even talked to Coach Meyer, Coach Olson had mailed me a bunch of information about Coach Meyer, including all of his records, experience, and a contact sheet that included John Wooden, Dick Bennett, Pat Summit and other high profile coaches that would attest to the quality of Coach Meyer. I don't remember even talking to Coach Meyer before I headed to school, but I remember being excited to play for a coach that had been successful and was so respected in the profession.

Meeting Coach For the First Time...

I can still remember the first time that I met Coach Meyer. The first day that I arrived on campus, I hooked up with my new roommate (and teammate) Sundance Wicks, and we moved everything into our dorm room in Jerde Hall. The following morning, Coach Meyer wanted to meet with both of us for the first time, and I remember that we both were pretty excited and a little anxious to meet him. Remember, Coach Meyer recruited neither of us, so this was going to be the first time we ever talked to him.

As we walked into his office, there was really no eye contact. The first thing Coach Meyer asked us is if we had notebooks and pens with us. Sunny and I both looked at each other questioningly and responded "no," which led him to ask us "why not?" That was one of coach's cardinal rules, to have something with you at all times to write with, so after we found some loose paper and a couple of pens in the office, we sat down and started taking notes. The thing that I still remember from that meeting was that as we sat and talked to Coach Meyer for probably twenty minutes, we never exchanged eye contact. I can't really remember what we talked about while we were in his office, but I do remember the last thing he said to us before we left. It went something like this: "Well, for all you know, I suck. And, for all I know, you guys suck. So, we'll just have to wait and see what happens." As Sunny and I walked out of that

15

meeting, I think we both were about the most confused that we'd ever been in our whole life.

Meeting the Guys...

One of my favorite experiences in not only my first year at Northern, but really every year, was meeting the guys. It was the most special that first year though, because it was the first chance that I was able to meet the guys that I would be going to war with everyday on the floor. Of course, the first person that I met was Sunny, being that we roomed together. The funny thing was that with a name like Sundance, I automatically assumed that he was Native American. I almost died when I saw this 6'5" skinny white kid walking into our dorm saying that he was my new roommate.

Another one of the guys that really stuck out in my mind was a player that had redshirted the year before named Nick Schroeder. Nick was another player staying in Jerde Hall with us, and he eventually became one of my closest friends. He was one of those guys that immediately welcomed you into the family and made you feel at home. Being in a totally new environment, it was crucial to have people like that, and Nick was always the type of guy to just drop by your room and hang out for hours on end. The other two guys that were a huge part of my life that first year were two of our seniors, Scott Hansen and Matt Sevareid. Both of these guys were point guards, which is what I played, so we immediately were connected in that sense, and they were just good guys more than anything else. Both of them were either married or engaged, and I can't even count how many times that first year they would have Sunny and I over for dinner or to just hang out and watch a game. When times got rough, and believe me when I say that they did that year, those two guys were always guys that I could count on.

Coach's Rules...

Coach Meyer wasn't the type of coach that sat us down and gave us a list of rules to abide by. He believed more in the concept of each player making good decisions, with the only real "rule" being that no player was allowed to do anything that would hurt themselves or the team. However, at the first meeting of each year, Coach Meyer would speak and he would always start off by giving us his three "rules." They are as follows:

1. Everybody takes notes
2. Everybody says "yes sir," "yes maam," "no sir," "no maam," (in other words, be courteous to everybody).
3. Everybody picks up trash.

The first time that Coach Meyer gave us those rules, I was just plain confused. I thought he would come into the meeting setting guidelines about partying, maintaining a certain GPA, and things like that, but all he had were three simple rules. First, everybody in the program, including the players, coaches, and student managers were required to take notes all the time. We were each given our own personal two-inch thick notebook, filled with nothing more than blank sheets of paper and a pen, and we were required to have that notebook with us at all times. When we met before practice, when we were on the road, when we were in the locker room before a game, and yes, even during the game, when we met before warm-ups and at halftime, we were required to take notes. Some people probably think that writing in a notebook during halftime of a college basketball games sounds a little ridiculous, but for our program, taking notes was simply a way of capturing memories and learning from our experiences, and being able to reflect

17

on those experiences. It's impossible for anybody to remember everything that is told to them over a period of time, but by writing things down, we were gaining an advantage over our competition, and we were learning a valuable life lesson. Coach Meyer would always tell us about a study that was conducted of the fifty or hundred wealthiest business-men in this country, and the findings showed that the only thing that all of them had in common were that they all took really good notes. Coach Meyer believed that successful people were good note-takers, and he made sure that by the time we left his program, we were all able to take good notes.

Coach Meyer's second "rule" dealt with courtesy. Coach Meyer was a stickler when it came to being courteous to all people, especially the ones that could do nothing for us in return (like children and the elderly), and if he ever found out that his players weren't being courteous, we were all going to pay the price. There is nothing fancy about this rule; it's just the right thing to do. Coach Meyer wanted good people in his program, and he expected us to be great people when we were off the court.

Coach Meyer's third and final rule was another simple rule. Just pick up trash. If you see a piece of trash on the floor, pick it up. It was that simple. For this rule, Coach Meyer led by example. No matter where he was, he picked up trash. He felt that this was another rule that simply dealt with common sense. I remember him being especially adamant about this in the locker room. In our locker room, he wanted us to take a lot of pride. Our locker room was like our home away from home, the place where we spent countless hours meeting, getting ready for games and practices, etc. and he believed that we should treat the locker room with a lot of pride. Even more importantly, he wanted every locker room that we used on the road to be in better shape when we left the room than when we arrived there. Coach Meyer would always be the last one out of the locker room, and he would watch to see that each player and coach picked up trash and cleaned the locker room before leaving. He felt that this was just another common courtesy that really took no extra effort and helped a lot of people, especially the janitors that would have to clean after the game. I remember seeing the visitor's locker rooms after they would leave our arena, and in many cases, it was just embarrassing. Towels were thrown all over the floor, trash was everywhere, sweaty ankle tape was lying on the carpet, and it really was ridiculous. I'm really thankful that Coach Meyer made us take the extra step to clean things up, because it reflects on our program. At Northern, we take a lot of pride in all aspects of the program, and cleaning locker rooms was no different. Sometimes Coach Meyer would read us a little note from a janitor at an opposing school who would take the time to write to Coach Meyer and thank him for the quality of the locker room after we left. Some people might think that this is just a little thing, and basically a waste of time, but in our program, we believed that the little things were the big things, and we at least tried to go the extra mile in everything that we did.

20 Minutes of Pain...

Throughout my five years in the program, I can remember doing some pretty brutal condition drills, but none was tougher than what we experienced during my redshirt year. At the start of the preseason, Coach Meyer wanted us to learn what getting in a stance was really like, and what it felt like to really sit in a stance. So, at the end of each conditioning session (we conditioned twice a week), Coach Meyer would have us sit in a defensive stance for a certain period of time. The drill was simply enough; each guy had to maintain a stance for however long Coach Meyer said, with all of the assistant coaches walking

19

through our lines and making sure that nobody cheated. If one person tried to quickly straighten his legs or cheat in any other way, the assistants would stop the drill, and we would start from scratch. It was definitely a drill to test our mental strength and our will power.

I think that the first day we had to sit in a stance for about three minutes, which seemed more like thirty minutes to us. Everybody made it through, but it was tough. When we finished, Coach Meyer merely said that we would go longer next time. The next time that we conditioned, we finished by sitting in a stance for five minutes. Then we increased to seven minutes and ten minutes. After we finished sitting in a stance for ten minutes during our second week of conditioning, Coach Meyer told us that by the end of the conditioning in a couple of weeks, we were going to sit in a defensive stance for twenty minutes; yes, twenty minutes. During each conditioning session, we would increase our time by a couple of minutes, and finally, we reached our last day of conditioning. After running sprints for a half-hour or so, it was time to go. We were allowed just a couple minutes to loosen the legs back up, and it was go-time. During those twenty minutes of pain, the only "break" that we got was Coach Meyer letting everybody stand up for ten seconds at the ten minute mark. He counted out ten seconds, and at the end of those ten seconds, we all had to be back in position. I remember the time barely moving. Eleven minutes, twelve, twelve-and-a-half, thirteen, fourteen, and so on. Finally, we were at about eighteen minutes, and we knew how close we were. Everybody's legs were completely numb at this point, and it was a matter of will power and doing it for the guy standing next to you. Every one of us wanted to quit, the pain was so excruciating, but we all knew that if we fell to that ground or stood up, every guy on the floor would have to go through it all over again. Finally, we heard nineteen minutes. We were all yelling at each other, encouraging our teammates, and just finding a way to get it done, when finally Coach Meyer yelled "Twenty Minutes!", and it was all over. Even though we could barely move, we were all hugging and celebrating like we had just won the national championship. We had survived Twenty Minutes of Pain. Every guy on the team found a way to do it, and being through such a brutal experience made us all closer. During each preseason we would always do something like that, a drill that was ridiculously tough and something that each guy finished or nobody finished, and it made us a stronger team. We knew that if we could sit in a stance for twenty straight minutes, we could do it for thirty-five seconds at the end of a game when we really needed a stop. Coach Meyer was building our mental strength and teaching us how to rely on our teammates.

The First Day of Practice...

Practice for NCAA schools usually begins around the 15th of October. With school usually starting at the beginning of September, basketball players have about six weeks of individual workouts, lifting, and scrimmaging before official practice begins. I can remember how nervous I was before our first actual practice. I really didn't know what to expect, but I guess nobody on the team did because it was the first time any of us had a practice with Coach Meyer.

Our first practice was actually an early morning practice at about 5:30 a.m. on a weekday. Practicing that early meant that we had to wake up at around 4:00 am because we had to be at the gym an hour early to tape ankles and loosen up before we hit the floor. Coach Meyer would be on the floor half an hour early helping guys with individual work, so when the actual practice time rolled around (in this case 5:30 am), we would hit the floor running.

21

All I can really remember from that first practice was sitting on the gym floor stretching beforehand, thinking that this was my first practice as a college basketball player. The excitement, nervousness, and butterflies that I felt in my stomach before Coach Meyer blew that first whistle were overwhelming. But, once we all hit the floor, everything pretty much evaporated except for playing the game. I have no idea what we actually did during that first practice, but I can remember the pace at which we moved in and out of drills. Coach is very similar to Coach John Wooden in that he is very precise in his practice planning, meaning that he has our whole practice mapped out from the second we step on the floor. When we moved from drill to drill, we ran. There was absolutely no wasted time, and if Coach felt that we weren't moving in and out of drills fast enough, we would just hit the line. I remember that sometime later in the day after that first practice, I got a call from my dad. All he said was, "Congratulations, son. You're officially a college basketball player." He was right.

Deciding to Redshirt…

After about the first two weeks of practice, Coach Meyer had a meeting with both Sundance and me, the two newcomers to the team, about whether or not we would be playing during the upcoming season. Incoming freshman have the option of taking a "redshirt" year, which meant that you practiced and traveled with the team, but you couldn't play in the games for the entire year. The upside is that at the end of the year, you are still considered a freshman eligibility wise, and when the next season kicks off, you still have four years of eligibility.

It was decided that Sunny was going to play and I was going to redshirt. As I mentioned earlier, I played point guard and we already had two seniors at the position, so it naturally made sense for me to sit the year, develop my skills, and get stronger in the weight room. Sunny, on the other hand, was needed right away because we had already lost one of our athletic wing players to a suspension, and Sunny was already prepared athletically to play at the collegiate level.

Even though it was logical for me to sit out my first year, I was not excited at all. Playing college sports is in a lot of ways a job, with all the time and other commitments that are involved. For me to put in that much work in practice and not be able to play in the games was a very difficult pill to swallow. Throughout that entire first year, I struggled to see the bigger picture, in terms of learning Coach's philosophy on the floor and developing my game and my body through the weight room and extra individual work on the floor, but when the year was over, I realized that it was the best thing that I could have ever done. I was able to learn from the sidelines how both our offense and defense was supposed to flow, I was able to watch how the point guard position was supposed to be played by two great players in practice and games, and I was able to increase my skill level. I really think that my redshirt year was the most important year of my career, because it built the base for my entire game and how I was going to fit into our scheme in the future.

Rough Spots in the Road...

My redshirt year is what I would have considered a transition year for our program. The coach at Northern prior to Coach Meyer was a phenomenal coach in his own way, Bob Olson. Coach Olson had been at Northern for a long time and had taken the Wolves to the NCAA Division II Elite Eight just two years earlier, and I think that Northern had won about the last five conference championships in the Northern Sun

Conference (NSIC), if not more, during Coach Olson's reign. The summer before I arrived to Northern, Coach Olson was offered the Athletic Director job at NSU, and he took the position, which opened up the coaching position for Coach Meyer. Sundance and I were actually recruited by Coach Olson, but by the time we came to school he was the A.D. and Coach Meyer was the new coach.

Going into my first season at Northern, I remember that we were preseason ranked #13 in the nation according to some magazines, so expectations were obviously high. Even with a new coach at the helm, it was pretty much assumed by all the returning players that "the sailing would still be smooth." This didn't turn out to be the case. Under Coach Meyer's beliefs, if you didn't work hard in practice, you weren't playing in the games, no matter how talented you were. By Christmas time, we already had two of our younger plays quit because they felt that they were better than some of the players getting minutes while they didn't see much time on the floor. Coach believed they didn't deserve time on the floor because their work ethic in practice didn't justify playing time.

As I mentioned earlier, in the preseason we were ranked as high as #13 in the polls, but I think that before we stopped at Christmas break, we were around 3-7 or at best, 4-6. Many of the older guys on the team were frustrated with Coach's different approach to the game, and for a lot of guys that had experienced a great deal of success in past years, things were not going smoothly. I remember that as we all left for about a three-day break for Christmas, the tension in the locker room was definitely starting to build.

All that tension finally came to a boiling point sometime in January when we were on a road trip for a conference game against Bemidji State (MN). After losing to a team that we supposedly hadn't loss to in many years, a couple of our older players, one being arguably our most talented player who was a

Preseason All-American, and the other being one of our senior captains, were allowed to drive back to Aberdeen instead of going back with the team on the charter bus. In some way, they abused the trust that was given, and they got in trouble. When Coach Meyer found out the next day, he gave them each a punishment that they felt was excessive, and they quit, so for the rest of the season we had eight players suiting, and one (myself) redshirting.

For the remainder of the year, our practices must have almost been comical to any outsider that ventured into the Barnett Center in the afternoon. We didn't physically have enough guys to scrimmage, so we had to put our managers and student assistants in the drills and scrimmages with us, just so we could have the numbers to play. A funny thing happened, however. The remaining nine of us that stuck with the program through all the bad times bonded into an extremely tight-knit squad. After the two players were suspended, our two senior point guards, Scott Hansen and Matt Sevareid, really took control of the team with their leadership and guided us the rest of the season. We immediately went on an eight-game winning streak going into our conference tournament, and we climbed up from about 8th in the conference to the 5th slot when the conference tournament began. I really thought that we were going to do some damage in the tournament, but just before it started, Matt Sevareid broke his hand trying to take a charge in practice, dropping us to seven remaining players. When we played in the first round against Southwest State (MN), we just didn't have the depth and firepower to compete.

We lost in a close game, and I'll never forget the feeling in the locker room after the game. There wasn't one guy in the room that wasn't crying, not really because we had lost the game and knew that our season was over, but because we all knew that the last two months of the season were something special and we knew that we would never have the same group again.

Sticking to a Commitment...

After our season was over, I had to really do some soul searching about what I wanted to with my college career. I had just finished my redshirt year, and it was really difficult for me. I also had a tough time adjusting to being so far away from home (about a ten hour drive), and it was difficult for me to get used to living in a town the size of Aberdeen (around 30,000 people), after growing up in Denver, Colorado my whole life. I actually was to the point where I felt that transferring was the best thing for me. Honestly, I wasn't mature enough at the time to see what a great opportunity I had sitting in front of me, and I felt that the grass was going to be greener on the other side, wherever that "side" may be.

Two people prevented me from transferring, and I owe everything to them. The first person was my Dad. I remember talking to my Dad many times on the phone after the season was over to talk about transferring schools. If it weren't for him I probably would have left. I constantly tried to convince him that transferring was the best thing for me, but he always came back at me saying that a man sticks to his commitments, even when times are tough. He let me know that the decision was mine and that he would support me either way, but he also let me know that if it were him, he would stay. I spent many nights thinking about his advice, and I was completely lost about what to do.

Even though I felt that staying was probably the right thing to do, I still wanted out. In fact, I was just about ready to talk to Coach Meyer and notify him of my plans, but I felt that I had to let my best friend know beforehand. Right after Spring

Break, I asked Sunny to go with me on a ride around town to talk about some things, and that is when I let him know that I was planning on leaving. I told him what I was thinking as we were driving, and then he stopped the car and said "Steve, if you leave, I'm leaving. We've talked about playing together all year, and it's going to happen. So if you really do leave, I'm gone too."

When he said that, I was floored. I didn't even know what to say. At that point, I realized how selfish I was. My whole focus was on myself, when my best friend was willing to do anything for me. I decided at that point to stick it out and totally immerse myself in the concept of the team, and stop worrying about myself. Like I said before, I owe everything to my Dad and Sunny. They are the ones that opened my eyes and kept me at Northern.

IN THEIR WORDS

Houston Reed, Northern State University
Player, Senior in 2002

My first contact with Coach Meyer came from a phone call in the mid afternoon as I was lounging in my dorm at Otero Junior College. The man on the phone began talking to me about all the fat pheasants he had been surrounded by for the last several weeks. I believe the last thing he asked me was if my shotgun had been polished lately. I finished listening to him not knowing exactly to whom I had just spoken. Little did I know these words came from a man that would impact my life in many ways.

Coach is a hard-nosed competitive man. He is a coach that is easy to play hard for because he leads by example. He puts all his heart, energy, and passion into his players. After Coach had his heart surgery, I remember him calling the basketball house to ask players to visit him on a more regular basis. A few times a week wasn't enough for him. He needed the interaction with his player's everyday.

Coming from the JUCO ranks I feel I have seen and heard some pretty wild things. But in a practice when Coach said, "If you don't play hard I'll kill you," I believed him (especially when he had that look where one eyebrow was raised over the other). Coach is a magnificent motivator and knows how to challenge each player to get the most out of him. What makes him a coach above all is he possesses that unique motivating trait. I would play for Coach any place, anywhere, anytime. I think he actually could have convinced me to run through a brick wall.

When you reflect on Coach's accomplishments, he obviously is classified with an elite group of coaches. When meeting and getting to know Coach, he has never acted like an elitist. His closest friends seem to be janitors, bus drivers, or event workers. He appreciates the work ethic of "blue-collar" people. He recognizes not what people do, but how they do what they do. He shows respect and dignity to people regardless of their social or economic status.

The beauty of Coach's accomplishments is how he has impacted the lives of so many: coaches, players, fans, co-workers, families, and supporters in the community. He is the true model for leadership. His passion for the game and for life rubs off onto all who are connected to him. He is a person that many aspire to be. He is a coach's coach as well as a player's coach. That is a feat not many have been able to accomplish. As players, our virtues and talents were all put into motion by our friend, mentor, and coach.

Barbara Anderson, Lipscomb University Secretary, 1983 -1999

I worked with Coach Meyer from 1983 until 1999 as his secretary at Lipscomb University. I always say that I worked with him, not for him because that's the way it was. He made me a part of the TEAM. He respected my opinion and valued my thoughts and ideas. He made me believe that I could do anything that needed to be done.

Coach has a tremendous work ethic and his desire to do things the right way made our basketball camp the largest

29

and best in the country. Every summer thousands of kids (some who could play and a lot that couldn't) attended our camps. They learned a lot of basketball and a lot more about life. Coach Meyer has impacted the lives of more people than anyone could imagine.

I had the opportunity to watch Coach with our players and student coaches for sixteen seasons. They all came in to the program as kids but left as men. What a blessing it was to me to watch as Coach taught them each day. I've seen him go nose to nose with some of our guys but I've also seen the hugs and smiles. I've witnessed countless phone calls and notes to former and current players. Coach cares about his players, he cares about their families, he cares about their jobs, he cares about their lives, and he cares about THEM.

I very much enjoyed being Coach Meyer's secretary - he is a man that I have a tremendous amount of respect for - a man who made a huge difference in my life - a man who truly cares about people. He is a great friend!

Brian Ayers, David Lipscomb University, Senior in 1993

As the son of a coach, I was fortunate to be around teams, games and camps from a very early age. My first exposure to Coach Meyer was as a camper the summer between seventh and eighth grades. It did not take long to realize there was something different and unique about Coach's program. At the end of the week, for example, there were no individual awards. I had grown accustomed to seeing hot shot champs, 1 on 1 champs, league champs, etc. walk away with trophies at other camps that I had attended. Now, on the last day of Coach Meyer's camp, I left with the same items as every other camper – a ball, a t-shirt and a notebook that all emphasized

TEAM ATTITUDE. As a camper you were a part of Coach's program and for that one week you were encouraged to "buy in" to his philosophy. Those who bought in left camp with more than those who found the discipline and the demands uncomfortable and not worth the effort. For those who left with a desire to be a better teammate, to play more unselfishly, and to work harder and smarter at the fundamentals, Coach had "reached."

The first time I actually met Coach was outside a locker room after one of our early games my senior season in high school. Coach's team had won the NAIA National Championship during my sophomore year and I was very excited that such a proven coach had come to watch me play. That first conversation began something like this: "Hey Brian…Coach Meyer…I think you could be part of a core group of guys that can compete for a National Championship…I liked the way you "worked" your warm-up." Like so many conversations with Coach there was not any small talk – just right to the point. Coach had emphasized the value of being on a team and the importance of work ethic from that first exchange and I would listen to him stress these convictions again and again over the next five years. From a camper to a recruit to a player the philosophy remained the same: put the team before yourself, always be willing to learn and be coached, and strive for excellence in everything you do.

One of my sincere hopes for my two sons is that they will come into contact with someone who will have as significant of an impact on their lives as Coach has had on mine. It may be a teacher or a coach or a relative or a boss. That will not matter to me. I just want someone who will challenge and push them. Someone who will demand what seems to be the unattainable. Someone who will make them strive for greatness. Someone who will make them do the right things for the right reasons. Someone like Coach.

31

Dustin Hjelmeland, Northern State University Player, Senior in 2005

When I started to think about what Coach Meyer has meant to me, what kept coming back up in my mind is all the life lessons he has taught me. When I first came to Northern as a freshman I used to get frustrated about how when we met how it was very rarely about X's and O's; it was always some quote or a bible verse that would help us to learn how to treat other people. I felt that this was a waste of time - I knew how to do those things, I knew how to conduct myself. But after looking back, I needed that much more than I needed to learn plays or to talk basketball. Don't get me wrong, Coach wants us to win and be successful just as much as the next guy (if not more) but he felt that it was more important that we focused on doing stuff the right way and that we focused on constant improvement, always trying to make ourselves the best we can be.

The trait that I most admire about Coach Meyer that I will always try to emulate when I start to coach is how he can be extremely hard, even ridiculing his players in every way possible, but he does it because he cares about them and is trying to make them better. Even after he's done getting after me for something I've done, I'm still thinking in the back of my mind how much he really must love me for him to care enough to challenge me that hard.

Just after watching for a day any outsider can see how much the team means to him and how he's always trying to make the team better. Probably the most important lesson Coach ever taught us was the importance of being a team. Being a team is the single most satisfying thing anyone can ever be a part of, to be involved in something greater than "you." When I came to the program all I could think about is how I could be the star, score and be able to play the most. I worked out hard but for very selfish motives. Coach helped me to realize the importance of doing it for the team. Now being a senior and seeing the end coming near, the question that I always ask myself is what can I do to help the others? In the words of Houston Reed before the playoffs in his senior year, "What can we do to make the season last longer so we can be together as a team just a little bit longer?" That really is what it is all about. And this is because of what Coach Meyer works so hard to instill in all of us every day in all we do.

Coach Meyer is a living example of how there are no short cuts in life and how doing the right thing like picking up trash will pay off for you in the end. While he has won many games, the most impressive thing is how many lives he has touched. In one way or another he affects every person he comes in contact with and his players lives are changed the most. Always pushing us to be our best and totally buying into serving our teammates the way our leader serves us everyday.

Thank you Coach!
Dustin Hjelmeland #34

Jason Shelton, David Lipscomb University, Senior in 1990

My days with Coach go all the way back to being a camper as a 5th grader. I attended basketball camp at Lipscomb for eight summers. It was the highlight of every summer for me. I guess that tells a little about how twisted I may be. This was during the days of the snorting Bison t-shirts and the tape on the tip of our shoes with your name facing out so your coach could learn your name better. It was at some point during those years I knew I wanted to be a Bison. I will never forget the day

I received a letter from Coach Ralph Turner (former assistant for Coach) stating that even though they had been recruiting me some they would not be able to offer me a scholarship but I could be a part of the team as a walk-on (I still have the letter).

While in school, I was part of some great years of Bison Basketball. We went 139-16 over the next four seasons. We were ranked #1 for two straight seasons. By saying I was part of some great teams I mean that my roles were different for every one of them. As a player my Freshman and Junior years, as a student coach as a Sophomore and then kind of a 2nd assistant coach while still a student for my Senior year and a 5th year while finishing my student teaching. After my freshman season Coach Meyer decided it would be better for me and the rest of the team if I became a student coach. I really don't know if he was more concerned for my health after an ankle injury or the health of my teammates that were real players that I might hurt in practice because of my lack of athletic body control. But during the fall of my junior year, I walked into Holman House (the basketball office) one day and I heard this from his office. "Jason, Go up in the attic and get some shoes, Snoddy will give you some practice gear and be ready to go today." There was not an invitation to play or even a "Hey we need you out there" kind of thing. As of that afternoon I was in charge of the "Red Team". The Red Team was our group of guys red-shirting or other walk-ons. We did scout team type things and worked like everyone else everyday. I wouldn't trade my last season on the floor as a player for anything.

There were no at large bids to the NAIA National tournament at that time. As hurtful as this story is, it must be told. During our junior season of 88-89 we were 38-1 and playing Belmont College in the game to represent our side of the Conference to go the tournament. Belmont had a great center just like we did named Joe Behling. To shorten the story I will skip to the half time speech. Coach Meyer was great at keeping us humble by staying on us when we were up and playing well; he would also be maybe a little more positive if we were playing another good team and just had not gotten it together well yet. Joe had 29 points on us in the first half. We could do nothing with him. They were playing well and we were playing pretty well also. One of the last things Coach said after a rousing half time talk was "He couldn't score 29 points in the 2nd half if we didn't guard him." Behling ended up with 58 and we were at home for the tournament. I will let you do the math on that one.

The stories could keep coming for days from my time as a player and assistant. Who will ever forget some of these from Bison lore: The famous Salad Bar & Water trip to Birmingham Southern, Chuck's speeches, Coach Chipman & Wolfie at Washburn, The Big Sandy incident, etc. but I will only give one more. One Sunday night practice around '96 or '97 Coach was in rare form. He was in a running mode and gave the command to "Just Start Running." That meant wherever you were you started running. There was no lining up and starting together and it usually meant it was going to last a while. So everyone is going all in different areas of the court. Coach proceeds to wax eloquently about the team's abilities. He had a ball in his hand at the time. During his words of wisdom he slammed it down with both hands for effect. As it came back up to him it kind of got into his kitchen and he mishandled it into the chin and chest. He didn't look the ball into his hands, block and tuck as we all know you have to do. That made him even more upset and caused him to punt the ball into the stands. As Coach went to plant his foot it kind of slipped. The ball shanked for a net gain of about 10 yards and Coach ended up on the seat of his khakis pants. All of us became the kid at church that just saw his buddy do something funny and couldn't laugh. There were lots of noises trying to fight off the laughs.

35

Three men have made me who I am today; my Dad, my Grandfather and Coach Meyer. I am eternally grateful for all he has done for me and so many others. Recently I became the Head Coach at Freed-Hardeman University, an NAIA school that was in our league before we left Lipscomb. When I interviewed for the job, I told them I wanted to do for other young men what Coach Meyer did for us. To me that would be a life fulfilled. A few months ago after Coach Meyer came to visit his in-laws in Colorado he spent a few days at our house. My son Mac said after he left, "Coach Meyer is my favorite coach in the whole universe." My response was "Mine too little buddy."

Thanks Coach,
Jason L. Shelton, '86-'91 DLU & '94-'99 Coach Meyer's Assistant

Tom Kelsey, David Lipscomb University, Senior in 1986

Probably no one has taken advantage and milked playing for Coach Meyer as I have. As a rising high school junior I took part in Coach Meyer's Bison Basketball Camp at David Lipscomb College in Nashville, Tennessee in the summer of 1979. From that first Sunday afternoon camp session watching a clinic by Mitch Kupchak (of the Washington Bullets) and Stan Kelner who was a guest lecturer on positive self imaging-.I was hooked. That night Coach did his goal setting session while some kids went to the Sunday night devotional in the Lipscomb cafeteria. That night I realized all this stuff that Coach put the campers through was incredible. Even as a 16 year old I realized that this was something special. Like most kids playing high school basketball I thought I would be playing big time basketball at the Division I level.

As I went into my senior year I once again attended the Bison Basketball Camp. After this summer session I was really hooked. In some crazy way the coaching staff saw that maybe I had some potential. I was invited to come back and work a week of camp and hang out with the Lipscomb players. To me at this age it was a little overwhelming and to me intimidating to be with the college players. I had an out because I was to attend the "B/C Basketball Camp" in Milledgeville, GA. This was back before the big Nike, Adidas and Reebok national invitational camps. As I competed as a camper that week Coach Meyer and one of his student assistants at the time (Billy Mooney) came to watch me play and to start the recruiting process. For me it was the beginning of an incredible teaching, playing and learning career.

For most of us that have played for Coach there is that certain intimidation process that we all go through. Not that Coach tries to intimidate; it is just part of the process. I know for us that played for Coach there is such a time that you may get over the intimidation and then it moves into a deep level of respect.

I think for us that go into coaching that is one of the biggest adjustments we have to make especially as a young coach. We think that if coach has that kind of respect we should immediately have that kind of respect. Through the years I have watched as so many former players have struggled with the point of wanting that immediate respect. When we do not get that respect right away we get upset. Imitation is a sincere form of flattery for sure and there have been numerous former players and coaches of Coach Meyer that have tried to imitate his coaching styles.

In my opinion here are few things that make Coach Meyer so good and what so many of us try to emulate.

37

His has the ability to instill confidence in his players.
"If I stop giving you instruction and getting on you, you better be worried"
He has the fascinating ability to teach the fundamentals of the game of basketball .
"Properly and quickly execute the fundamentals of the game"
He has an ability to make it really about the people.
"If it is a choice between you and the program the choice has already been made"
His ability to look at the "Big Picture"
"It's not what you achieve, it's what you become"
As Coach Meyer always says: *"Be what you is, because if you be what you ain't, you ain't what you is"*

Thanks Coach for being who you are and not trying to be what you weren't - Tom Kelsey

2000 − 2001:
"ROLES: DEFINE, UNDERSTAND, ACCEPT, FULFILL"
FRESHMAN YEAR

The Tennessee Trip...

When summer finally arrived, Coach Meyer had given each of the teammates the opportunity to work his camps that he still ran in Tennessee. With Coach Meyer coming to Northern so late in the summer the previous year, he still had camps that he ran in Nashville, where he was previously coaching. Most of the guys didn't even consider going to the camps, being that they were all the way across the country and the pay wasn't very good. But Sundance and I talked about it and decided to give it a try. We didn't have any summer jobs, and we liked to take trips, so we went for it. We decided to work the first week or so of camp in Nashville, and then two of our upperclassmen, Brad Hansen and Jake Phillips, were to come down and work the second week of camps.

I remember Sunny and I driving from Aberdeen to Nashville, which is almost a twenty-hour drive. It was on trips like that where we became such close friends. We had a great time going down to Nashville, but we had no idea what to expect when we arrived. We had heard that Coach Meyer's camps in Tennessee were some of the largest in the country, and being around Coach for the past year, we knew that his camps probably weren't the type of camps where the campers just played games the whole time. For Coach Meyer, camp was an opportunity for players to get better, and he made them work. Being at those camps was such a great experience for me because I saw young players that loved to work hard at improving their skills. Coach Meyer, the other top instructors, and all of us workers in general took the camp very serious, and the campers loved the intense approach.

There was one incident in camp that I'll never forget and it's an incident that I think made Coach Meyer realize that I was going to be a mentally tough player, if nothing else. At the end of each night, Coach Meyer would gather all of the campers, from young players to high school seniors, in the central gym to watch demonstrations by the college players. Being that Sunny and I were the only two college players from Northern at the camp, we did a lot of the demonstrations. The camp was pretty large, and as I recall, there were probably around 200 to 300 campers sitting under the main basket watching demonstrations. On the first night, Coach Meyer had Sundance come out first, and he had him demonstrate some shooting drills and things of that nature. Sundance was coming off of a great freshman year, where he was the NSIC Newcomer of the Year, and he had proven to Coach Meyer that he was a player. I, on the other hand, was coming off of a freshmen year in which Coach and I battled a lot over me being too flashy of a player (Coach would always call me "California Cool") and I hadn't proven anything to Coach Meyer in terms of being a player in a game-like atmosphere. With a gym packed full of interested campers, Coach Meyer had the perfect opportunity to see how I would handle his intensity and yelling.

Coach Meyer had me do a shooting drill where I had to just shoot until I made twenty three-pointers. It was a simple enough drill, but I was about as nervous as I had ever been. I was to shoot, and Sunny was to rebound and pass out to me. I started shooting and I couldn't hit anything. After a minute of shooting, I maybe hit three or four shots total. The whole time, Coach was just screaming at me, yelling things like, "Steve, you better learn to make your shots, because I'm not letting you shoot more than two a game next year!!" I can still hear him in that gym. I finally made my twenty three-pointers, and it took me awhile, maybe five minutes (which seemed like an eternity) but I didn't give up. When I was shooting, I didn't react to Coach's yelling or start making faces, I just kept shooting. And even though I put on a miserable shooting demonstration for those campers, I think that Coach saw that I would compete even when things weren't going smoothly. I believe that Coach took note that I was willing to do whatever it took to be a better player. Shoot, of the fifteen or so guys that we had on our team, only four guys made the Tennessee trip, and Coach notices things like that. I believe it was during that camp that Coach realized that I was really committed to being a good player and more importantly, a team player.

Learning & Understanding my Role...

After sitting out for an entire year while redshirting, I couldn't wait to start my freshman season. I had been in the program for a year and had a much better idea of what Coach Meyer wanted than when I originally arrived at school. Going through all of my internal struggles during my first year, I was finally focused on being a part of the program and being more concerned about the importance of the team. The team concept finally started to "click" for me. I understood that I was only a very small part of a much bigger team, and I was excited to start the year. I knew that with both of our point guards from the previous season graduated, there was going to be a chance for me to get playing time. Coach had signed a very talented

41

point guard from Texas, a Division I transfer named Roland Williams, so I knew that if I was going to get playing time, I would have to find a way for Coach Meyer to put me on the floor.

In that first year, my "role" on the team started to develop. Coach Meyer would always talk about everybody having a certain role on the team. He would say "Roles: Define, Understand, Accept, Fulfill." What he meant was that for each person individually on the team, he would define a specific role (some guys had the role of scorers, some guys had the role of passers, screeners, etc.), the players had to understand what their role was, the players had to accept their role (which wasn't always easy for a lot of guys), and they had to then go onto the floor and fulfill their role. It took me probably at least another year to really see the big picture and understand what my role on the team would be, but I started to understand what Coach Meyer expected from me and all of the point guards on the team. As a point guard, I was to initiate the offense, keep things running smoothly, be a great defender, and make no stupid mistakes. Coach Meyer wanted his point guards to truly be an extension of himself on the floor, and as a point guard, I knew that Coach would demand a lot from me if I was going to be able to get playing time.

A Whole Slew of new Guys...

By the end of my redshirt year, we had eight guys remaining to play and myself. Because of players quitting throughout the year, we were extremely shorthanded. Both of our point guards were seniors as well, so by the time the season ended, we only had seven guys that would be back for the following season. The coaching staff had to bring in a lot of players, some that would be freshman and could possibly redshirt, and the remaining players being junior college guys that would come in with two years of eligibility remaining. Throughout the course of my career, Coach Meyer rarely recruited junior college players (in fact after my freshman year, he only signed one more in the next three years), and I think the reason was that for most players, it took at least a year to be comfortable in Coach's system of play. By the time the players were comfortable and ready to go, they would already be seniors, and by that point, Coach Meyer would usually play a younger guy that had more time to develop.

But, being that we didn't have any numbers for the current season, Coach Meyer signed three junior college players that would be ready to help the team immediately, along with four freshmen that would hopefully be able to develop for the future. With so many new guys on the team learning the system and trying to find where they fit into the big picture, it took a long time to develop a team that had specific roles that worked together to form that "big picture." We were coming off of a season with a final record of 13-14, and we wanted to win now, but it took a long time to form the team and style of play that Coach Meyer wanted.

Taking Notes …

One of the ways in which Coach Meyer differentiated our program from probably almost every other program in the country was that he had his players keep a notebook full of practice notes, theories, game concepts, and life lessons. At the beginning of each season, the coaching staff would hand each player a 2" thick notebook with a stack of blank paper, and we were required to have our notebooks with us every time we practiced, played, or met as a team or with Coach Meyer individually. If we had a team meeting and a player forgot his notebook, Coach was not happy.

We mainly used the notebooks either before or after every practice. Usually, after we finished a practice, we would all go into our locker room, with our chairs in the shape of a circle, with everybody facing Coach Meyer. We would discuss his notes from practice, what he felt that we did well, and what we needed to work on. We would diagram our plays and different sets, with Coach Meyer drawing them on the board, expecting us to also draw them in our notebooks. Coach would also give us phrases, not necessarily about basketball, but usually about life. I can remember him saying, "Mistakes: Recognize, Admit, Learn, Forget," "We practice and play with the poise of a national championship team," "Roles: Learn, Define, Understand, Accept," "There comes a time when winter asks what you've done all summer," "You can't fake the harvest," and countless others. I could go on for days repeating some of the quotes that Coach Meyer would say to us. And he expected us to write everything down.

I remember complaining in my first couple of years, not understanding why we had to keep writing the same things down, time and time again. It would take me a couple of years and a lot of growth in the area of personal maturity to understand why Coach would stress and repeat the same sayings over and over. But one day, the light finally came on, and I realized Coach Meyer was preaching about more than basketball in those meetings. He was teaching us about life. And by forcing us to write things down, he was giving us an invaluable tool that we could refer back to for the rest of our lives. There was no way that we could have remembered even a fraction of the things that Coach taught us during our days as players on memory alone, but by writing everything down, we had in essence a "basketball bible," full of the ideas of one of the most knowledgeable coaches in America, and we also had a personal book full of life lessons. I review my notes constantly to this day, as I try to learn how to coach and teach the game, and I'm grateful that I have such a great book to guide me. As I look back, those sessions were some of my favorite times as a player because I was learning about so much more than basketball. I was learning about life.

My first collegiate experience...

After redshirting for the past year and going through two straight preseason conditioning sessions, I was ready to play. I couldn't wait to finally get on the court and just play the game again. I thought going into my first game that everything would be similar to when I played in high school, and I didn't think that I'd have any troubles adjusting to the speed of the game, but I remember that I was so nervous before our first exhibition game that I couldn't stop shaking.

We were going to play an all-star traveling team called *Pella Windows* at the Barnett Center at NSU. The first game had finally arrived. I didn't care that it was an exhibition; I just wanted to be on that floor as soon as possible. I didn't start the game (or any other during my freshman year), so I had no idea when Coach Meyer was going to call for me to go into the game, but when it finally did happen and I went up to the scorer's table, I felt like a frightened child. All I could think about was not screwing up, which is obviously the last thing a player should do in the heat of the battle. Either way, when the whistle stopped play, I checked into the game and my career had begun.

I didn't really do anything in my first game in terms of making shots, or getting assists, or anything else for that matter, but after the game I felt relief that it was over. All the anxiety and excitement that I felt going into the game was now gone, and I knew that after I played a couple of games at the collegiate level I would be able to feel comfortable and focus on the game. The main thing that I still remember from the first game was how fast it seemed to me, and how much bigger the players were. Even though I had been practicing with our guys for a year, nothing can really compare to a game in terms of speed and the physical nature of the game, and my eyes were opened.

Pepsi Classic...

Our first two games of the non-conference season were to be at a tournament in Mankato, Minnesota called the Pepsi Classic. In our first game, we played a very good team, Grand Valley State (MI), and after being down by more than twenty points at halftime, we made a serious run in the second half, but still lost 89-82. I didn't play much during that game as the backup point guard (maybe 10 or 15 minutes), and after the game, I was still frustrated that I wasn't adapting to the speed of the game. Things were still happening too quickly for me out there. I wasn't making good decisions as a point guard, and it was frustrating.

Our second game of the tournament, against Bellevue (NE) was a different story, however. We were able to get a large lead on Bellevue from the opening tip, and Coach Meyer played me a lot, especially in the second half. I responded by having eight assists and only one turnover, and after the game, Coach Meyer selected me to talk on the post-game radio show. What a difference twenty-four hours can make! I had gone from really struggling just one day earlier to being the guy selected to talk on the radio because I played well. My parents heard the broadcast after the game and I remember how excited they both were. It was a great feeling to have played well and to have experienced my first collegiate victory. The best part about the whole game was that I finally felt comfortable again on the floor. I wasn't rushing or trying to force anything in our offense, but instead, the game had finally slowed down.

Christmas Break (4-6)...

After the Pepsi Classic, we had a couple of victories in Aberdeen (vs. Chadron State [NE], 101-73 and vs. Rochester 106-81), and then we lost four straight over the next couple of weeks. As Christmas rolled around, we were sitting at 4-6 overall and 0-2 in conference. Most of our victories had come against teams with sub-par talent, and we weren't at the level to compete with the top Division II schools in the area (South Dakota State, who was usually ranked very high nationally, had just defeated us 99-78 before the Christmas break). Either way, when we came back from Christmas, we were to begin the bulk of our conference season, and everybody on the team was anxious to see how we would do.

Southwest State...

By the time we traveled to play one of our biggest rivals, Southwest State (MN) in late January, we had a record of 8-8. We were beginning to play better with each game, but we still had a long ways to go. At this point in time, I was beginning to find my "niche" on the team, playing a little under twenty minutes a game, shooting open threes if they were available, trying to play the best defense that I possibly could, and running the team with (hopefully) as few mistakes as possible when our starting point guard was taking a breather. Coach Meyer was beginning to feel maybe a little more comfortable

47

when I was in the game, and because of that, my minutes were increasing as the games went on.

The Southwest State game was one that I have never forgotten, not because of how we played, but because of an incident that happened to me during the game. Midway through the second half of the game, the score was very close and Coach Meyer put me into the game. This was a very intense game against a hated rival, and the pressure in the gym was mounting as the clock wore down. A couple of minutes after I checked into the game, we had the ball on offense and with the shot clock winding down, someone passed me the ball on the perimeter. Instead of shooting the open shot, I tried to drive the lane and ended up turning the ball over. Coach Meyer was irate. He immediately subbed me out of the game for not shooting the open shot, and as I came off the floor near the scorer's table, Coach was waiting for me. He was yelling that I should have shot the ball, and then, he sort of popped me on my side with a right jab. Coach Meyer didn't hit me that hard, but just the fact that it happened kind of stunned me and I sort of keeled over, right in front of the scorer's table in full view of the more than 3,000 fans that were in attendance. I walked to the bench to sit down and I have to admit that the only word to describe how I felt was "stunned." I was embarrassed that all those people saw it happen and I just didn't know what to think.

Most of our players on the bench didn't see it happen and had no idea what was going on, and I didn't want to say anything during the game, so I just kept my mouth shut. Coach Sather, our assistant, put me back in the game with a few minutes left, and I was like a zombie on the floor. My mind was racing in a million different directions and I just wanted to get out of the gym. After the game, we all went back to our locker room, and I remember waiting for Sunny. I saw him, pulled him aside, and tried to tell him what happened, but I just lost it, and started crying. He didn't see anything during the game, so I'm sure he was wondering what the problem was, but finally I was able to let it out. As a team, we all met after the game and Coach Meyer talked about the game (which we lost) and that was it. I was hoping internally that the incident would just die there, and that we could move on, but I doubted that was going to be the case.

After the game, many of the parents and the fans came up to me and asked me if I was all right. Sure enough, they had all seen the incident, and they were upset. I had parents telling me that they were going to call the athletic director, and do this and that, but I just wanted to have it dealt with between Coach Meyer and myself. My parents weren't at the game (which was a good thing, because my mom probably would have charged the bench), so I guess all the other parents were just looking out for me as though I was their child. That's how close the family is at Northern. Anyways, I finally was able to make it to the bus, and eventually, some of the guys started asking me what happened during the game. Before we left, Coach Meyer walked to back of the bus (which he never does) and talked to the whole team about what had happened. He apologized to me and I could see how sincere he was about it. I could see that it was killing him inside because of what he did, and I just wanted the whole thing to end right there. We had a big game the following night against Wayne State (NE) and the last thing that the team needed to worry about was me.

The Next Night...

We traveled to Wayne, Nebraska that night and settled in at the hotel. While there was a sort of "awkward tension" among the guys during practice the following morning, everything was pretty normal. After going through our regular game-day

49

rituals, we arrived at the arena to watch the first half of the girl's game before heading to the locker room. My parents were coming from Denver to watch the Wayne game, and I hadn't talked to them about what had happened, so I knew that when they arrived, I would have to mention the incident to them. They were at the girl's game when we arrived, and I was able to sit and talk with them for awhile, eventually telling them what had happened on the previous night. My dad, being a high school coach for a long time (and probably feeling the same urge to pop a player from time to time) took the news pretty well, but mom was a different story. She was upset, to say the least. She didn't want to hear about Coach Meyer popping her youngest child in the ribs, but she remained cool, and I think my dad eventually calmed her down. Halftime approached, and we headed for the locker room to get ready for the game.

The Wayne State game was a huge game because we hadn't beaten them at their place in about four years, as our assistant coach, Coach Sather, emphasized before the game. In addition, we weren't happy with our performance the night before so we wanted to really play well. The first half was knotted up the entire time, with neither team able to create any separation. I think we might have had a two or three-point lead at the half, but it was close. The second half was the same story, with neither team able to take a strong lead, and with about eleven minutes left in the game, our starting point guard, Roland Williams, was charged with his fourth foul, so I was sent in. I was still a little shaky emotionally from the night before, but I went in the game confident. When I got in the game, we started to play really well and I was able to get a couple of assists, hit some big free throws, and play some solid defense against one of their top players, so Coach Meyer kept me until the end. This was a big turning point for me because this was the first time that I was in the game late with the outcome still in jeopardy. We ended up winning the game 75-70 and it was possibly our biggest win of the season up until that point.

I was so glad that things turned around and that going home on the bus we were able to focus more on the win than on the events of the previous evening. I was able to see my parents after the game, and Coach Meyer actually talked with them beforehand, telling them what had happened and apologizing for everything. That's one thing that makes Coach Meyer so special. When he makes a mistake, he admits and corrects it. So many people are afraid to do that, but not Coach Meyer. He knew that he shouldn't have hit me, but people make mistakes. I had already forgiven him, and I'm sure that my parent's also had by the time the bus left Wayne State.

Conference Tournament...

Going into the conference tournament, our overall record was 14-12, and we had the fifth seed (out of eight teams), which meant that our first round game would be on the road against the fourth seed, which happened to be the University of Minnesota-Duluth. We knew that it would be a tough game in Duluth, and they had beaten us both times that we played earlier in the season, but we felt that we could definitely win the game. In terms of talent and athleticism, both teams were similar, so we liked our chances.

We battled the entire game, giving a great effort, but it just wasn't meant to be. We ended up losing 87-78, and for the second straight season, we were eliminated from the tournament in the first round. It was really tough losing that game, because we had a couple of seniors that we were all going to miss. We all wanted to win because of our competitive nature, but we also wanted to win because we knew that the longer we played in the tournament and into March, the longer we had to be a part of the team. Once we lost that last game, we would never be able to play with the seniors again. The team the following season would be different, and so we tried to play as long as possible to keep our team together. We really liked each other that much.

Postseason Meetings...

Every year, about two weeks after our last game, Coach Meyer would schedule individual meetings for each one of the players. He wanted to talk with each of us about our strengths and weaknesses, what we needed to work on in the spring and summer to improve our games, and how life was going outside of basketball. Coach Meyer was very blunt in the meetings (as was the case all the time). If you needed to get stronger, Coach was going to let you know. Coach's approach was to be honest and to the point, not worrying about the feelings of the player, because he wanted to see improvement. If he babied us as players, we wouldn't push as hard as we did to become better. Coach knew that sometimes "medicine is hard to swallow, but needed for the body to repair." Coach was going to tell the player what type of "medicine" he needed to improve his game, because Coach Meyer was a competitor and wanted good players.

My individual meeting with Coach Meyer that year is something I will never forget because of what he told me. After the meeting began, Coach Meyer talked about the fact that he felt I had really improved throughout the year and that I could really contribute next year if I kept working on my game. He knew that I was a self-motivated player, so he didn't have to try to "push my buttons" to make me work harder in the weight room, or spend more time working in the gym; he knew that I would do that on my own. What he did do in that meeting was tell me the most straight-forward, honest comment that I think anybody has ever told me. Coach said, "Steve, I just want you to know that you'll never be all-conference. For us to be a good team, you may play a lot in the future, but you won't ever be an all-conference player."

When he told me that, I was obviously upset, because I had an ego. Deep down, every player loves recognition and awards, and ever player wants to be "all-conference." I didn't understand why he would even say something like that, and it took me probably two years to understand what Coach was talking about. Once I figured it out (in the coming years), I realized what Coach Meyer was doing. In that meeting, Coach Meyer was laying the seeds in my mind as to what type of player he wanted me to be. Coach wanted me to be a pass-first type of player, a guy that does all the dirty jobs, is hopefully the best defender on the team, and doesn't mind not getting recognition. In fact, for Coach Meyer to tell me that I wasn't going to be all-conference was actually a compliment, because he must have felt that I could be mature enough to handle that type of role. At the time, I left the meeting thinking that he didn't want me to succeed, but when I became older, more mature, and maybe just a little wiser, I realized that he was trying to set me up to be a big part of truly great teams.

Summer Camps...

There was never really an end to our season at Northern. In the fall, when we arrived at school, we immediately started individual workouts, lifting, and conditioning. Obviously, our normal season was during the winter months, and in the spring, Coach Meyer had us right back to the individual workouts and lifting that would improve our skills. This is a typical pattern at most collegiate basketball programs, but one are where we differentiated ourselves was during the summertime.

As I mentioned earlier, when Coach Meyer was coaching in Tennessee, he ran some of the largest summer camps in America, and after his first year of transition between his old school, David Lipscomb, and his new school, Northern State, he had prepared to move his summer camps to Aberdeen. We usually ran about seven different types of camp throughout the summer, with the first block of camps beginning in late May and ending in mid June, and the second block of camps going a couple of weeks in July. I think that I can say that our camps are probably unlike any other camp in America because of how Coach Meyer approaches the camps and, in turn, how he runs them. Coach Meyer took summer camps very seriously, and after the first couple of years, the only people that would come to our camps were those players that were extremely serious about learning the game and improving their skills.

For example, Coach Meyer required every camper and every coach / instructor to have a notebook and always be writing when we gathered as a group. It didn't matter if the camper was a second-grader or a coach that had been in the business for twenty years, everybody took notes. There were no games played in our camps, with the whole day comprised of individual skill development and fundamental work. Camp usually started at 6 am for the early birds and campers weren't released back to their dorms until just before 10 pm, so it was work. By the end of the three-day session, the campers (and us players) were extremely tired, and although a lot of them complained throughout the week that the camp was too hard and that they just wanted to play games, when they left for home, they all felt that they had the tools to start to become better players. That was exactly Coach Meyer's goal.

That first year of camp was a special year because as players, we had never been exposed to what Coach Meyer expected during the summertime sessions, and it was an eye-opener for us. First, even though we weren't "required" to stick around during the summer, we all knew that it was a foregone conclusion that Coach Meyer expected every player to be in Aberdeen during the camps. In addition, Coach made us work. In a lot of the other camps that I've worked at when I was a player and now as a coach, I've never seen players so focused during camp. Most of the time players just have to ref a couple of games, sitting under a basket and collecting a paycheck. That wasn't the case with Coach Meyer. He would always be watching us to see if we were doing a good job, and if we weren't he would let us know about it. Coach Meyer took so much pride in the camps, and he wasn't about to let his players slack during them. After we realized what kind of impacts we could make on younger players that looked up to us as college players, we took a great deal of pride in the camps as well. Whenever Coach Meyer made us demonstrate a drill for the campers, we wanted to do it as near perfect as possible, because we had a lot of pride and we didn't want to look bad in front of a group of 200 campers. It was really true that Coach made us take pride in everything we did, and camp was no exception.

Another area in which Coach Meyer differentiated the idea of a summer camp was in the types of camps that we had. We had a camp strictly devoted to college players (which I haven't seen anywhere else that I've been), we had two boarding camps, a week of day-camp, and a specialized shooting camp, a camp devoted to post players and perimeter players, and finally, the Coaching Academy. While all of the camps offered a different "flavor," the Coaching Academy was my personal favorite and was in many ways the most exciting camp for us players. Coach would always bring in one or two high-profile Division I coaches to headline the two-and-a-half day session, and for the first year, Tennessee Volunteer's coach Pat Summit was the headliner. As players, we served as demonstrators for all of the coaches (for example; Coach Summit, Coach Meyer, our assistant, Coach Sather, etc.), and we had to demonstrate various drills, sets, plays, etc. in front of the hundreds of coaches in attendance. I would personally say that the Coaching Academy was more pressure on us players than a big game during the year. With all of those coaches in attendance expecting to see a good demonstration, we players knew that we had to be on top of our games to give a good demonstration. Every year, at least a couple of players would just freeze out on the court, but it was understandable. We really wanted to give a good demonstration. People paid good money to come to the Academy, and we wanted them to go away feeling that their money was well spent.

IN THEIR WORDS

John Pierce, David Lipscomb University, Senior in 1994

I remember the first time I ever met Coach Meyer. I was a sophomore in high school and was going on a date with his oldest daughter. I went to their house to pick her up, and as we went into the living room I saw him lying on the couch watching TV. His daughter said, "Dad, this is John." Coach Meyer made no move to sit up or greet me, but instead remained on the couch and grunted. Needless to say, I was a little intimidated after meeting him for the first time. Little did I know that I would spend 5 years learning from him about basketball and more importantly about life.

Coach Meyer was obsessive about "the little things." How you caught the ball, how you pivoted in the post, your hand position in the post, your foot position when defending the ball, your routine at the free throw line. These were all detailed things that he taught us in practices and games. More importantly he was obsessive about the "little things of life." From Coach I learned the beauty of helping someone who could give you nothing in return. In fact, Coach seemed to shy away from the political aspect of being a college coach. He was definitely not one to "kiss up" in order to get what he wanted. He was constantly surrounding himself with people who would not and could not advance his career. I think of all of the people like

Chuck Ross, Denita - one of his secretaries, area high school and junior high coaches, as well as countless others.

Coach taught me the art of being involved in community. Our community consisted not just of the coaches and players, but also the student assistants, the secretaries, and the managers. It was very important to him that we were a team; that no person on the team, himself included, was more important than any other member. We faced the challenges and the successes of each year as a community, bound together by a common cause.

A couple of stories about Coach – to say that he is cheap is like saying that the sun is warm. I remember seeing him driving one day and all of a sudden stopping on the side of the road. Watching him, wondering what in the world he was doing, I was not shocked to see him get out of the car, reach down in the grass, and grab an empty Coke can. He would retrieve empty aluminum cans from all over Nashville to get a few cents. He may say that he was cleaning up the environment, but we all know he just wanted the 2 cents per can. Along those same lines we were on a road trip to play a game in Jackson, TN. We had stopped to eat our pre-game meal at Shoney's restaurant. Before we went in, Coach gave us specific orders about what we could get. We were able to each get a salad bar and water. Nothing like feeling energized for a game with a nice piece of lettuce in your stomach.

Needless to say I owe a great deal to Coach Meyer. I honestly feel his knowledge of the game of basketball is unsurpassed, and I appreciate the rich education I got about the game. But, more than that, I am grateful to him for his heart for people, for his willingness to give his life to his players, for his generosity and compassion for others. I am thankful to have played for a man who had an ability to break the game of life down to the "little things" that really do matter.

Tony Birmingham, Northern State University Player, Senior in 2005

First, and probably the most obvious, is that Coach Meyer is a *teacher* above all else. He is someone who teaches young men or boys to grow up and become men so they can survive on their own or enable themselves to provide for their family. He does this by what some may refer to as the Socratic Method. He gives the player assignments and then he tests that player on those assignments. He teaches his players the fundamentals of the game and then he tests his players in numerous ways to see that they are keeping up on their progress. Coach Meyer is someone who accepts nothing but someone's best attitude and effort.

There are many coaches and people who can say one thing but then don't have the commitment to see it through and stick with it. Well, not Coach; he does not care what the final score of the game was, he does not care who won or lost, his main concern is that the attitude and effort of the players are the best they have to give. He will not accept anything less. He is not afraid to let his players know when their actions are not on par with his expectations either. A mutual respect is developed almost immediately and the player must both be all in and trust that coach is doing things to benefit the team or get out because it will be a long haul for both parties otherwise. The one thing that always amazes me about Coach Meyer is that he is able to retrieve facts and teaching points for games or situations that occurred long before many of his players were even born. He is extremely wise and sharp and is always looking for new and more proficient ways to keep his edge. There is a saying that goes something like "you can tell the character of a man by the company he keeps." I think this would be self explanatory in terms of Coach Meyer. The never ending lists of

59

friends and fellow coaches he has is unbelievable, names such as John Wooden, Pat Summit, Coach K, Morgan Wooten, Dean Smith, Bobby Knight etc.

To conclude, Coach has had an impact in my life much like a parent has on their child, but in a much shorter time span. Coach expects greatness from you and expects you to expect it from yourself. Coach has had a life altering impact on me personally. Sure you will never be able to tell that from my box scores or my stats, but hopefully the way I treat people and the character I show in the future will help keep Coach's lessons alive. As Coach says, the true test of a man's character is how he responds to a challenge. Coach Meyer challenges me everyday and even though when I am done he will no longer physically be there, his lessons and challenges will continue to be an intricate part of my life.

Greg Glenn, David Lipscomb University, Senior in 1986

Coach Meyer has had as strong of an influence in my life as anyone I've ever met. It would be difficult to describe how different I see the world because of my experience in the basketball program at Lipscomb. Somewhere between the intensity in which Coach lives each day and the sincerity in which he treats each person that is fortunate enough to have crossed paths with him is what makes him so unique to me. His capacity to share and use what he has either learned or is learning to make himself and the people around him better is amazing. I've never been around anyone who motivated me more to be my best in every area of my life than Coach. Because of his insatiable desire to improve, his methods might change but his message stays the same; "Leave the place better than you found it." Coach continues to do that in his own special way.

Greg Glenn
Lipscomb '82-'86

Bob Olson, Athletic Director, Northern State University

There is so much you could write about Coach Meyer. I really don't know where to start. When I think of Coach Meyer, thoughts such as these go through my mind--team, loyalty, coaching for all the right reasons, developing players and young men, and a passion for the game of basketball.

Coach Meyer has the conviction and strength to run a program as it should be run. His athletes are very disciplined, on and off the court; as well as around the campus and in the community. Coach is a student of the game and always on the "cutting edge" of his profession. Coach Meyer is a definite team player and supports all athletes in all programs. Coach Meyer is strong enough to do the right thing, no matter how it affects the scoreboard. The student-athletes that Coach Meyer recruits to NSU are always recruited carefully. Athletic ability is important, but not at the expense of a reasonable chance of academic and social success.

In closing, I would like to express what a pleasure it is to work with Coach Meyer. His passion for coaching, for working with student-athletes, and helping fellow coaches is second to none. We, at NSU and in the entire region, are very fortunate to have both Coach and his wife, Carmen, as a part of our community.

Wade Tomlinson, David Lipscomb University, Senior in 1990

"CHARGING @ AQUANIS"

In the pre-season of my senior year we had a scrimmage game against Aquanis Jr. College. On this fall afternoon we were part of and witnessed another part of Coach's legacy.

During the scrimmage one of our teammates missed an opportunity to take a charge. Right at this moment Coach became slightly irritated, grabbed the ball and started spitting and yelling that no one would take a charge. He then proclaimed that no one was man enough to take a charge from him. He started running towards the five guys that were out on the floor and lined them up to take a charge from him. First was Jerry Meyer. Jerry took a forearm to the neck. Next was a forearm shiver to the chest of Pete Froedden. Tracy Sales and Daren Henrie wilt and collapse before Coach gets to them. When Daren went down he fell on his side and Coach got tangled up in his legs and tripped where all of his momentum, and forearm, was heading into Philip Hutcheson's chest. While this was happening I jump up off the bench yelling expletives and heading for Coach, wanting to take a charge. Jason and Coach T practically tackled me and told me to cool down. After they wrestle me back to the bench I proceeded to take my shoes off (because Coach was always saying "when you're done leave your shoes in the locker"). I then toss my shoes out on the floor and walk out of the gym. Thank goodness Coach never heard or saw any of this and that Jason picked up my shoes! Needless to say the crowd and the other team were totally stunned. In the crowd were the Campbell's and Pierces. They had come over to see Mark and John during their redshirt year. Thank goodness their parents did not make them transfer.

There are five things that could have brought this reaction from coach. I will list them from least likely to most probable. A. Someone did not step in front of the ball and take a charge. B. The pressures of again being preseason ranked # 1 and returning several players was getting to Coach. C. He believed that physically we had no testicles and he was trying to promote some type of hormonal growth. D. Coach being Coach! Or E. All of the above.

Wade Tomlinson
David Lipscomb University
1986-1990

Drew Gruver, Northern State University, Senior in 2002

The first words Coach Meyer said to me when I went on my recruiting visit were "You look like puke." What was I supposed to say to that? I knew I was skinny and didn't have the best body in the world, but most people would at least say hi, or nice to meet you first. Not Coach. After that we went out to his house and watched "What About Bob," his favorite movie. Or so he said. I don't know if that is a fact. From then on the rest of my visit he called me Bob Grover. My last name is spelled G-r-U-v-e-r and my first name is Drew. He would even call in the summer and leave messages on my answering machine asking for Bob Grover, and if my Mom or Dad answered the phone he would ask for Bob. I wondered what I had gotten myself into. It turned out to be a good thing.

I have a lot of great memories of playing for Coach Meyer. I was a Junior College transfer and played two years for Coach Meyer. The things that really stood out to me from the beginning were his attention to detail, how much he cared about the team, his players, and the game of basketball. Coach Meyer is a great teacher of not only the game of basketball, but more importantly, the game of life. I learned a lot about both in the two short years I played for him. I will always remember the TEAMS I was a part of at Northern State and how lucky I was to play and learn from one of the best.

Drew Gruver
Pride In The Pack! (2000 – 2002)

2001-2002:
"FINALLY FEELING COMFORTABLE"
SOPHOMORE YEAR

Coach's Heart Surgery & Josh's Suicide...

In the summer of 2002, life was moving along in a routine fashion. In mid-July, we finished our last camps, and there was about a month or so left before school started. Most of the younger guys were back at home spending time with their families, and some of the older guys that now lived in the team house, like me, Sundance, Nick Schroeder, and Drew Gruver were still in Aberdeen. Time was just moving along as always until two phone calls changed my life.

For the first phone call, all of us guys were sitting at the house probably watching television or just hanging out, when Coach Meyer called. Coach Meyer would rarely call us at the house, so we knew that it was sort of strange. But when he called, he had us all get on a couple of separate phones, and he told us that he was going to be undergoing a major heart surgery. Apparently, almost all of his arteries were clogged up, so he was to undergo (I believe) a "five-bypass" heart surgery in Sioux Falls, SD in about a week. He assured us not to worry, that it was a pretty standard operation and that he had an excellent surgeon performing the surgery, but nevertheless, we were all a little bit worried.

A few days later, on a Saturday morning I received another

phone call from my Dad back home in Denver. As soon as I got on the phone with him, I could tell that something wasn't right, and he told me the following words; "Son, I just received a phone call. Josh just killed himself." I didn't really comprehend what he had just told me. Josh was one of my best friends back in Denver, part of our group of guys that had always been together in high school, and a great kid. He was a college football player, loved by his friends, one of the funniest guys I had ever known, and out of nowhere, I get a call that he had killed himself? I didn't understand, and I definitely couldn't comprehend what had just been told to me. There was to be a church service the next morning and then a funeral the day after, so I threw a bunch of stuff in a bag and got ready to leave. Sundance was in the room next to me, and I'm sure that he could hear me talking, and after I put the phone down he was in my room asking me what happened. He had met Josh a couple of times when he was with me in Denver, and he wanted to know what he needed to do. He was ready to get in the car with me if that's what I wanted, but I had to go home and deal with the tragedy on my own. Within a couple of minutes I was on the road driving home, and during the entire ten-hour drive I never knew what I was thinking. My mind was racing a thousand miles per hour and at the same time I was thinking about nothing at all. I was numb.

I made it home and dealt with the funeral with my family and friends from back home, and a couple of days later I had to go back to school. At the same time, Coach Meyer was undergoing his surgery in Sioux Falls, South Dakota and I hadn't even heard how the surgery went because of what I was going through. But, when I got back, two incidents happened that I will never forget. The night that I returned Coach Meyer wanted all of the guys to come to his house, eat some dinner and just hang out. Everybody was curious to see how he was doing, and everybody knew that I was really struggling, so it was good to bring the team together. So we went out to Coach's house, ate our usual hamburger meal, and then hung out in his game room playing pool and watching television. During this time, Coach Meyer called me over to go on a walk with him outside. I'll never forget that walk. Coach and I walked just out in front of his house, just so he could talk to me in private to see how I was handling my own tragedy. When I looked at him talking to me, I could see a row of stitches that went all the way up his leg and I could see that he was in bad shape, but the only thing he was concerned about at that time was me. Coach Meyer had just undergone a life-threatening surgery a couple of days earlier, and in all honesty, he probably shouldn't have been walking outside at all but he knew that he needed to talk with me and comfort me. That's why Coach Meyer wasn't just my coach, he was my friend.

The other incident happened the next night during a typical summer scrimmage at the gym. By now, most of our guys were back, probably about twelve of us, so we went to the gym to get some games in. During the games I think that everybody could see that I was still struggling with my issues, and I just wasn't playing well at all. My head and my heart weren't into it. After awhile, I just sat out and let some of the younger guys play, and when I was sitting on the sideline watching the guys play I couldn't stop thinking about Josh and I just started crying. One of our seniors, Houston Reed, saw me on the sideline and he, being the leader and friend that he is, stopped the games, came over and just hugged me. Soon enough, all of the guys were there, hugging me and trying to help. We weren't just teammates; we were all best friends in our program. When one of us had a problem, it was everybody's problem, and that's why we were so incredibly strong as a group.

The First Meeting of the Year...

The first meeting of the year was always a special time. The entire team had just made it back to Aberdeen before classes started, and we were all excited to get another season started. No matter how old I was in the program I was always nervous and excited for that first meeting. The meeting would always last about an hour, and at the start of the meeting we would all receive our notebooks. By the time Coach Meyer started speaking we were all writing.

I believe that the first meeting of the year dictates the expectations and attitudes of the program for the entire season, and so when Coach Meyer began to talk, he wasn't smiling. Even though I'm sure he was excited to finally get the season started, I think that if he was smiling and joking during that first meeting, the new guys in the program would think that he was always that way, and so he came in with a scowl on his face and a glare in his eyes.

As players, we could feel the electricity in the air. I remember always thinking in those meetings about how good we could be as a team. Could we win the conference title again? Could we make it to the national tournament? Nobody knew the answers at that point, but I always wondered how good we could be. I also wondered about which guys were going to step up in the program. We all knew which guys stayed in Aberdeen over the summer, and who was working out to improve on their game, but nobody would be able to tell who really improved until we started workouts and scrimmages. During that first meeting, Coach Meyer would tell us his three rules (take notes, courtesy, pick up trash) and he would talk about the upcoming season. He would stress leadership (who would be our leader this year?), he would talk about getting in the gym when we weren't required to, and he would talk about the importance of the next six weeks of preseason conditioning and training before official practice began. After the meeting ended, it was time to go. The season had officially begun, and now it was time to start working.

The Fire Drill...

I'm not sure when or where Coach Meyer picked up this conditioning drill called "The Fire Drill," but it was tough. Any time we were having a bad practice or sometimes just to finish off the practice, Coach Meyer would call for two lines at half court facing opposite ends, with the lines each containing half of the players. The player at the beginning of each line would have a ball in their hands. When the whistle blew, both lines had to start running towards the hoop that they faced, with the first player tossing the ball off of the backboard. Once the balls hit the backboard on both ends of the floor, the next player would have to get to the ball before it hit the floor, again toss the ball off of the backboard, and so on, until the drill was over. After a player reached the front of the line and tossed the ball off the backboard, he had to then sprint to the other end of the floor, getting in the next line of players, where the same action was happening at that hoop. In essence, once the drill began, it was like the players were almost running in a circle from one end of the court to the next, with two balls that could never hit the floor once they were tossed off of the backboard.

Now, many teams that I know of do this drill for conditioning. It is actually a pretty well-known drill for basketball teams, and it makes the players work hard, because if one of the balls does hit the floor (if a player doesn't make it in time to keep the ball alive) the drill starts over. In fact, some people reading this may be wondering why this drill is even mentioned. Well, just like in many other areas of our program

Coach Meyer wanted to go a little further with the drill to make it tougher on us, and he certainly did. Not only did we have to run to each end of the floor from line to line before the balls hit the floor, Coach Meyer created some more guidelines to make it tougher on us and make us more disciplined. First, during the entire duration of the drill, he made us run with our arms pointed straight up with our hands toward the ceiling. If Coach Meyer or one of the assistant coaches saw anybody on the team bend their arms at all the drill started over. The drill usually lasted for around 3-5 minutes, so you can imagine how sore a person's arms and shoulders would get during that time (for fun, try holding your arms straight up right now for three minutes, it's not easy). In addition, everybody on the team had to be talking and encouraging their fellow teammate for the duration of the drill. And we had to be loud. Coach Meyer would sometimes even send a student manager or coach outside of the gym and into the hallways to see how loud we really were. If the student manager came back and said that he couldn't hear enough talking in the hallway, we started over.

Finally, instead of just throwing the ball up against the backboard so it hit the backboard and then running to the other end, Coach Meyer required us to have the ball hit above the top of the square on the backboard (on each backboard, there is a square that is approximately 12 to 16 inches in each direction, so we had to have the ball hit at least 16 inches higher than the rim). Then, instead of just sprinting down the middle of the floor, which is obviously the shortest distance on the floor, Coach Meyer wanted us to simulate a fast break situation where we ran the floor "wide" so he would have us players run outside the "Wolf ears." We had two wolf emblems on our floor near half court and very close to the sidelines, so when we ran outside the wolf ears we were running as close to the sideline as possible learning how to run a fast break properly, with our wing players spread out.

Sometimes when we were running the drill, and it felt like my arms were about to fall off, I would silently wonder why Coach Meyer made us do all of the extra things. Why did we have to talk as loudly as possible? Why were we running with our arms above our heads? We would never do that in a game. Why did we have to make sure the ball hit above the top of the square? For me, it just didn't make much sense at the time. But once I got a little older and started to learn how to think more like a coach, I realized that Coach Meyer was teaching us so many lessons. First, he was teaching us to play through pain. By the end of the drill, we were tired. But when a player gets fatigued, he or she can't quit talking or doing the little things like running outside the wolf ears. Coach Meyer was teaching us that. He was also teaching us pure discipline. We had to do a lot of things in that drill perfectly, or we would start over. It was tough enough for one guy to remember to do everything perfectly, but when you factor in that we usually had at least fifteen guys on our team, then the drill became real interesting. Coach Meyer was also teaching us individual responsibility and collective dependency on one another. If one guy didn't feel like talking, we all suffered. If one guy dropped his hands for a second, one of the assistant coaches was going to see and then we all would suffer. So Coach Meyer was teaching us "to do it for the guy standing next to you," as he always said. Looking back, the Fire Drill wasn't even a conditioning drill; it was a team-building drill. There are a million different drills a coach can run to get his players in shape, but how many coaches take that extra step and demand that their players do the little things, show discipline, and learn to count on one another during a drill like that? The Fire Drill is just one of the things that we did to separate our team from other teams, and I believe that by the time we finished a drill like that, we were closer as a team.

"Echo Calls"...

One of the things that Coach Meyer demands from every player on our team is constant communication on the floor. Whether we were at practice, in a four-man individual workout, or during the middle of an intense game, Coach Meyer expected us to talk to each other. Coach would always say "A quiet team (gym) is a scared team (gym)," and it made a lot of sense. I always noticed as a player, and now as a coach, that as the pressure increased in a big game and the crowd became louder, the majority of the players that were nervous or scared would first lose their ability to talk. I'm not sure why that is, but for whatever reason when the stakes are high in a basketball game most of the players automatically go into their own little world, and communication evaporates between teammates. Coach Meyer knew this, and he wanted to make sure that we were always communicating on the floor from the first day that we became a part of the Wolves tradition.

One thing that I've found out as a coach is that it's not easy to get a whole team to talk. Sure, there will always be one or two guys on the team that are more vocal than the other players by nature, but the majority of the players never want to talk. I think it's assumed that the point guard should be able to talk and communicate to his or her teammates (the point guard is like the coach on the floor), and it's probably also assumed that the team "captains" should be good communicators, but what about the other twelve to fifteen guys on the team? Shouldn't they have to talk? Coach Meyer would always say that "On a good team, one or two players do the dirty jobs, but on a great team, everybody does them." I think the same applies to talking; "On a good team, one or two players do all of the communicating, but on a great team, everybody communicates."

So how did Coach Meyer teach us to communicate as an

entire team? That's a good question, and let me assure you that it wasn't easy. Coach Meyer would institute a "concept" into our practices that he called "Echo Calls." Echo Calls simply meant that whenever a coach or player yelled out for the team to change drills (for example, we might be in a shooting drill and then an assistant coach yells to change into our partner passing drill), every single player on the team had to echo that call. If we heard a coach yell "Partner Passing!" we all, as a team, had to yell "Partner Passing!" Although it sounds simple enough, this was in fact very difficult. Most of the time we were focused in whatever drill we were doing, and sometimes we didn't hear the yell or whoever initially made the call didn't yell loud enough, and thus, the echo call wasn't perfected. If every single player and coach in the program wasn't screaming out the call, then Coach Meyer would simply put us on the line and we would be running. Coach would tell us to start running lines, and as we were running at some point he would again make a call for the drill, and we all would echo him, sprinting into the next drill.

During the early stages of the season Coach Meyer would test all of the players, especially the freshmen, so that they could learn how to talk. Most of the time we would be in our partner passing drill spread across the floor, and as we were doing a specific pass (for example the right-hand flick pass) Coach Meyer would walk up to one of the freshmen and whisper "left-hand flick pass." That player would then have to yell "Left-Hand Flick Pass!" for everybody to hear, and if we didn't echo the call we were back on the line running sprints. Here is the key point that Coach Meyer stressed: If the freshmen didn't get the call communicated, was it only his fault? Of course not. There was surely one or two other players close enough to Coach Meyer that also heard him make the command, and they should have also been yelling "Left-Hand Flick Pass!" Coach Meyer wasn't just teaching us how to simply talk as a team; he was teaching

73

us how to be good teammates. As he always said, "If one of us fails, we all fail."

The Season Finally Begins...

Finally, the season had begun. We were all excited to get things under way, and we all felt confident about how we were going to do as a team throughout the season. In the past two years, we had records of 13-14 and 14-13 respectively, and we felt that we finally were going to be able to really compete with the top teams in NCAA Division II. We had most of our players back from last year's team, and everybody was starting to understand what Coach Meyer expected from us as a team and individually. I felt like I had personally matured a lot, and I felt like the guys were starting to trust me more as a point guard. From the beginning of the season I was the starting point guard, and I finally felt like I was ready for the position. I was beginning to feel more confident in my abilities to be a point guard at the collegiate level, and I couldn't wait to see how we would do as a team.

We started the year off with the three straight blowout victories over NAIA opponents (79-55 vs. Jamestown, 85-50 vs. Mount Scenario, and 113-57 vs. Dakota State), and then we had to play three consecutive games against very good teams from the North Central Conference. The North Central Conference was one of three conferences in our region, the North Central Region. Our conference (the Northern Sun), and the Rocky Mountain Athletic Conference were the other two. Across the nation, the North Central Conference was considered to be one of the toughest conferences every year, and our conference, the Northern Sun, never received the same amount of respect as the other two leagues in the region, so when we played games against the NCC in the preseason they were very important games to show that we could compete against the top teams in the country, not just the teams from within our conference.

Our first NCC game of the year was to be against North Dakota State University, and we lost a heartbreaker in Fargo, North Dakota by the score of 70-68. That game was followed by another NCC contest against St. Cloud State (MN), who was ranked 8th in the country at the time. It was played on our home floor, at Wachs Arena, but it didn't matter as we were handled by the more athletic Huskies by a score of 84-68. That game was followed by another NCC contest in Brookings, SD against one of our in-state rivals, South Dakota State University. At the time, they were ranked #12 in the country, and we were again outmatched, losing 95-81.

UND...

We followed up the NCC swing with our first two conference games, easily beating Concordia-St. Paul (MN) by a score of 84-35 and then beating a good Winona State (MN) team 77-71. The following week we beat a non-conference foe, the University of Sioux Falls (SD) in a blowout 99-69, and we had one more game before the Christmas break. We were to play our last non-conference game, against yet another powerful NCC team, the University of North Dakota. In my three years in the program up to that point, we had yet to beat a team from the NCC and we knew that if we really wanted to gain respect outside of our league, on both a regional and national level, this was a must-win game for us. UND had a very talented team, and one of their players, their 6'10" center Jerome Beasley, was actually drafted in the second round of the NBA draft after graduating by the Miami Heat.

In terms of size, athleticism, and depth, we were outclassed

75

by the Fighting Sioux, but we felt confident that we could compete with them if we stuck to our game plan. The game was played in Aberdeen on our floor, and we knew that we would have a big crowd that night. I don't remember the specifics of the game, but I do remember that early in the game, we were down by a score of about 18-3. UND was just crushing us on our home floor. Beasley had already caught two alley-oop dunks, and things weren't looking good. Coach Meyer kept us calm, however, and by halftime we had closed the gap to single digits. In the second half, we continued to chip away, and about midway through the period, we had our first lead. We continued to play our kind of basketball, and with only minutes left we broke the game open, eventually winning 80-65 and improving our overall record to 7-3.

Now, in terms of the big picture, the UND win shouldn't have been that big of a deal. It was just one game, and it wasn't even a conference game, so it really shouldn't have meant a lot. In fact, we felt that we were every bit as good as UND was, so it shouldn't have been a surprise to us when we beat them on our own floor. But, even though it wasn't necessarily a surprise, it was a huge win nonetheless. For the first time in three years, we had finally beaten one of the "mighty NCC" schools, and that did a lot for our confidence. In addition, it was the last game before a week-long Christmas break, so while we were back at home during the break every player on our team was beginning to believe that we could win big games and compete with the best teams, not only in our conference, but also in our region.

The Season Progresses...

Coming back from Christmas break, our remaining games were all conference games, and we were excited to get into the conference season. We started off with two straight road wins, beating Wayne State (NE) 77-67, and Southwest State (MN) 72-62, upping our record to 9-3, 4-0. We split our next four games, beating the University of Minnesota-Crookston and Bemidji State (MN), and losing to Minnesota State-Moorhead and the University of Minnesota-Duluth (our overall record at this point was 11-5, 6-2). And then we really went on a roll, winning five of our next six games, bringing our record to 16-6, 11-3 in conference. At this point, we were in second place in the conference, trailing only the University of Minnesota-Duluth for the league lead with only four games left in the regular season. It was the best record that we had achieved since I had been at Northern and everybody was talking league title.

Our last two home games of the year were to be rematches against Bemidji State, who was tied with us for second place in the league, and against league-leading UM-Duluth in our final home game of the season, but before we could even prepare for those games we had one more road game against Minnesota State-Moorhead, who had already beaten us at home earlier in the year. Moorhead had a very good team and we knew that it would be very difficult to beat them on their floor. Early in the game the lead continued to switch hands, and neither team could get control of the game. It was very physical early on, even to the point where we felt that some of their players were taking cheap shots. Sure enough, with about one minute left in the first half and right in front of our bench, one of their players tried to take a cheap shot on our freshmen guard, Jarod Obering, and Coach Meyer saw it happen. Coach Meyer just lost it, yelling at the player who was involved, and yelling at the referee who either didn't see it or didn't make the call. Soon enough, Moorhead's coach saw Coach Meyer yelling at his player, which turned into him and Coach Meyer yelling face-to-face at half court in front of the scorer's table. Moorhead's home crowd, which was a pretty decent-sized crowd, went into

77

a frenzy and basically it was a scene of pandemonium. Finally, the refs restored order and the first half quickly finished. We all ran into the locker room, and before our coaches walked in we came together as a team. I'll never forget Houston Reed, one of our seniors and easily our toughest player, yelling at each guy on the team, saying that nobody does that to one of our guys, nobody! He had my attention, and I know he had everybody else's attention. When Houston started yelling, which was not often, we all listened. And then Coach Meyer came in.

When Coach Meyer and the other coaches came into the locker room, the first thing he did was calm us down. He made it clear that we were going out in the second half to win a ball game, nothing more. He assured us that the crowd would be crazy, and the intensity in the gym would be very high, so we were going to have to match their intensity step for step, but that we must remain calm and composed. He never liked to bring emotion onto the battlefield; he felt that it would hurt our focus. But then, Coach Meyer got "the look" in his eyes, and he basically said the same thing that Houston said to us before he got in the locker room. He made it clear that nobody takes a cheap shot at one of our guys and he made it clear that this was one of those times where we had to take a stand as a team. It was up to us.

When we came back out for the second half, the crowd was indeed crazy. In fact, the security guards on duty at the game had to spread out in front of the student section, standing between them and the court, just in case things escalated again. We were ready to go, and as the second half began we were able to match Moorhead in terms of intensity. At the same time, we did a really good job of keeping our composure, and as Coach always liked to say, we played with "cold-blooded execution." We were precise in everything we did and we won the game running away 80-64. It was a big win in terms of us being mature enough to not only step up to a challenge, but also to keep our poise in a very intense road battle. It was also a big win because we knew that if we won both of our games the following weekend, we would have our first league title in three years.

The League Title comes down to the Final Weekend...

We had three games remaining; our last home weekend against Bemidji, who was in third place in the standings, and Duluth, who was now tied with us for first place (we both had identical records of 12-3), and our final conference game at Minnesota-Morris, who was in last place in the league. Our first game was against a very athletic Bemidji State team, a team that was very different from us in terms of their style of play. Our team strength was our inside play (our starting center Brad Hansen was eventually named NSIC Player of the Year and was named a Division II All-American), so we tried to jam the ball inside on basically every possession, whereas Bemidji was an athletic, three-point shooting team. I believe they finished the season ranked #1 in the nation in 3-point shooting, and they tried to push the tempo by shooting quick shots on offense and pressing on defense. It was definitely a contrast in styles. When we first played Bemidji earlier in the season our style of play prevailed, as we easily beat them 93-69 on their own floor, but we knew that they were a dangerous team and very capable of beating us.

We were all excited going into the Bemidji game. We felt real confident that we would be able to take care of business on our home floor after already beating Bemidji at their place, but we also knew that with the level of talent on their team, anything could happen if we didn't play well. I'm not sure what really happened during the game but we came out flat and we

79

never found a rhythm throughout the entire game. Bemidji didn't play that well, either, but we continually made defensive lapses, and as the final buzzer sounded, we had lost 79-76, losing out on a chance to be the sole league champions. We were all disappointed as a team and Coach Meyer was definitely upset, not because we had lost the game (Coach Meyer always cared much more about how we played than if we won or lost) but because we were so sloppy throughout the game.

Nevertheless, we had to play again the following night against Minnesota-Duluth, and we still could win a share of the league title if we won the game. The Duluth game was the final regular season home game of the year, which was always a special game. It was Senior's night, Parent's night, and a special night for the fans, called I Hate Winter, all bundled together. It was usually the game that drew the most fans (usually around 5,000 or 6,000 depending on the game) and being that it was a game to determine the league title, we knew that the Barnett Center would be packed. Earlier in the year, Duluth had handled us pretty easily at their place, beating us much worse than the 79-72 final score indicated and we had actually lost to Duluth the last four times that we had played them, so we knew that it would be a challenge to pull off a victory.

On that Saturday night, I'll always remember us running into the gym for warm-ups before the game. The place was packed. The official attendance for the night was over 6,300 people, each fan trying to cheer us on to victory in such an important game. I could personally feel the intensity in the building that night; it was the first time in three years that we were playing for a league title, and after winning the league title for five consecutive years (from 1995-1999), our fans wanted to see us put up another banner in 2002. Most players don't get a chance to ever play in an atmosphere like that, and I just remember feeling excited to be in that gym on that night. Before we came out for the final introductions we came together in the locker room one last time, and I could tell that everybody was ready for the game. We were all pumped, but we were poised at the same time. Coach Meyer said a few final words, and it was time to go.

What I can really remember about that game was one of the first plays after the opening tip. About one minute into the game (I don't think that either team had scored yet) there was a loose ball situation on our defensive end of the floor. The ball squirted loose, and I ended up with it. As Coach Meyer had always taught me, my first look was down the floor to see if we had an opening for an easy lay-in and sure enough, one of our post players Andy Foster, was lumbering down the floor with nobody else in sight. I fired a full court bounce pass to him, and he finished the play with a monstrous, two-handed dunk, sending the crowd of over 6,000 into frenzy.

As the first half progressed, we started to gain the momentum, continually trying to feed the ball inside into our All-American center, Brad Hansen, and our backup center (and another very good player) Andy Foster. When the final buzzer sounded to signal the end of the first half, we found ourselves leading Duluth 33-19, with Hansen and Foster scoring 16 of our 33 points. We felt very good about how we were playing, but we knew that Duluth would make a run in the second half; we just hoped that we would be ready.

Sure enough, early in the second half Duluth found a rhythm on offense and they began to chip away at our lead. We continued to feed the ball inside with success throughout the second half, but Duluth continued to gain ground and with just under five minutes to go in the game, Duluth finally caught up to us on the scoreboard, tying the game at 55-55 for the first time since early in the game. In the final four and a half minutes there were seven consecutive lead changes, with one team hitting a jumper to take a one-point lead, and then the other team tying the game on the following possession.

Everybody in the gym knew that the league title was going to come down to the final possession, and sure enough, it did.

We were leading Duluth 60-59 with forty seconds remaining when they hit a jumper to take the lead 61-60. In this type of situation, most coaches would immediately call a timeout to set up a play, but Coach Meyer never called a timeout, letting us players handle the situation on the floor. I believe that he felt confident enough in our abilities as a team to let us deal with the situation. I remember bringing the ball down the floor and looking inside for Brad Hansen, who was always our first option. He was guarded well and so I went to Sundance to see what he would do. Sunny couldn't find an opening in the defense, swinging the ball to Nick Schroeder, our three-point specialist, as the shot clock was winding down to five seconds and counting. Nick caught the ball, faked a three-point shot on the left baseline, took a dribble to the side and shot a pull-up from about sixteen feet. The whole thing happened in slow motion for me. It felt like once the ball released his hand, it stayed in the air forever (with the league title on the line) but soon enough, I saw the ball seamlessly swish through the net, and the crowd erupted, as we took a 62-61 lead with fourteen seconds remaining. Nick had a knack for hitting crucial shots when we really needed them, and once again he had come through for us in the clutch, drilling a shot that potentially was going to win us a share of the league title. But there was still time for one more play for Duluth. We knew that they were probably drawing up a play for their best player, Chris Stanley, who already had 23 points on the night. When the ball was set into play, Duluth hustled down the floor, immediately going to Stanley. Stanley made a move, and then pulled up for a game-winning jumper. Again, time seemed to slow almost to a halt, but as the ball made it to the rim, it bounced off to the side. Sundance rushed in for the rebound, and was fouled with only a couple of seconds left. He hit one of two free throws, and

Duluth never got off a last shot. The game was over; we had won 63-61, beating Duluth for the first time in over two years and basically claiming a share of the league title after having a record of 27-27 the previous two years.

We had one last game to play before the playoffs to officially claim a piece of the league title, a road game against Minnesota-Morris, who was standing in last place in the league standings. There was no way that we were going to slip up and lose a chance at the league title, and we played well, crushing Morris by a score of 94-66. It was official. We were league champions, sharing the title with Duluth, with both teams having a league record of 14-4.

Winning our first league title...

After we beat Morris and it was official that we were going to be league champions, I was just ecstatic. One of the things about playing at Northern is that everybody always talks about the teams that have won league titles and put banners on the wall and went to the national tournament, etc. I always wanted to be able to put at least one banner on the wall of the Barnett Center, so when I came back to Northern years down the road, I could look at the wall full of banners and say that I was a part of at least one of those teams. Coach helped us to understand that basketball and more specifically, our program, was about more than just putting banners on the wall, but being a very competitive person I wanted to at least have one of those banners on the wall. In addition, to win the league title after struggling the past two years, with so many players leaving the program during our first season and so many "fair-weather" fans losing faith in our program and Coach Meyer after being spoiled with the success of the past, it felt really good to be back on top. I was really happy for Coach Meyer. He had to

83

take a lot of heat during those first two years because we weren't winning and because he shipped some of our problem players off the team, and I felt like he deserved the championship. I was proud of all the guys that had been there for those previous two seasons and had stuck with the program and with Coach Meyer. It was nice to be a part of that group of guys.

NSIC Tournament...

Even though we were excited about winning the league title we knew that for us to make it to the national tournament we had to win the league tournament the following week (or hope to be chosen as an "at-large selection," which wasn't likely in our league). We found out that we were going to be the #1 seed in the tournament because of a tiebreaker that we had over Duluth, and our first opponent was to be Minnesota-Morris in the first round. We went into the tournament with a record of 19-7, 14-4 in conference.

The first round of the conference tournament was always played at the home of the higher seed, so our game against Morris was to be played in Aberdeen. We had no problem with Morris, playing them for the second time in five days and beating them easily by a score of 99-47. We were moving on to Minneapolis and the Ganglehoff Center (where the semifinals and finals of the tournament were played each year) for the first time since I had been a part of the program. Our opponent was going to be Southwest State (MN), the #4 seed and a very dangerous team. We had split victories with Southwest State during the regular season, so we knew that it was going to be a war.

As I just mentioned, we had never played in the conference tournament at the Ganglehoff and while the crowds weren't nearly as large as the ones that we played for in the Barnett

Center, the intensity of playing in a tournament game in a packed, little gym was huge. I could tell that we were all nervous, maybe because we were the #1 seed and hadn't been in that position before, and maybe because we knew that we had to keep winning to advance to the national tournament (even with the 20 wins that we had, it was doubtful that we would receive an at-large bid). The start of the game was sloppy on both ends of the floor, but after a couple of minutes both teams calmed down, and the game was underway.

About halfway through the first half, in a very close game, we were pressing full court on their end of the floor when one of their players lost the ball. I was in the area, and diving on the ball, I looked up and saw Houston Reed flashing down the lane towards the basket. Houston was about 6'7" and he just wasn't the most athletic guy. In the two years that we had played together, I had never seen Houston dunk the basketball one time (in practice, games, or any other time), but as he ran through the lane, I hit him with a pass and out of nowhere, BOOM! Houston crushed in a two-handed dunk, exciting and shocking our crowd and all of us players at the same time (adrenaline can do funny things). As the first half progressed, the lead continually changed, and at halftime, we went into the locker room down 36-34.

The second half was much of the same story. After we started the half with a lay-up by Brad Hansen to tie the score at 36-36, Southwest regained about a five-point lead and for the remainder of the game we continually battled back, but we just could never capture the lead. Every time we made a run Southwest would answer and for the majority of the half, they held between a three and seven-point lead. However, with just minutes remaining we made one final run chipping away at their lead. We were down 66-62 with two minutes left, and Sundance drove the lane, missing a lay-up. He quickly got his own rebound, making the follow-up and cutting the lead to

66-64. We were back in business. Southwest came down the floor and in the open court, our forward Drew Gruver made a clean steal, taking the ball the length of the floor and making another lay-up, and finally the game was tied 66-66. I was sure at that point that we were going to pull off the victory. The momentum was in our favor and Southwest was finally backed on their heels after leading for the entire game. There was about one minute remaining.

Southwest came down, working the ball inside, and they drew a foul. Their center Chad Koenen went to the free throw line and calmly sank two shots, giving them the lead at 68-66. We came down the floor with the same strategy, pounding the ball inside to our center, the conference MVP, Brad Hansen. Brad made his move, went up for a shot, and Koenen made a great play blocking his shot, getting the rebound, and getting fouled. Koenen came down and made one of two free throws, increasing the lead to 69-66 with 51 seconds remaining. We still had plenty of time, so instead of forcing up a quick three-pointer, we again went inside to Brad. He made a great move, but he missed a difficult shot and Southwest gained control of the rebound. I fouled their player immediately and their guard, Jimmy Dekker, calmly sank two free throws increasing the lead to 71-66 with only thirty seconds remaining. We called a timeout to draw up a play for a three point shot, but when we came down, the shot was missed, and Southwest made all of their remaining free throws, ending our chances at winning the game. The final score was 77-70, and our season was over.

We didn't get an at-large invite to the national tournament, finishing a very good season with a record of 20-8. Even though we had a good year, we were very disappointed to be done playing. We felt that we had earned a chance to be playing in our regional after winning twenty games (one of the at-large selections was a team from another conference that had only won 17 games during the year), but our conference didn't have the respect that we felt it should, and we were left out. It was a tough pill to swallow.

The Learning Program...

I believe that one of the biggest differences between our program and most of the programs across the country at all levels was the fact that Coach Meyer was more of a teacher than a coach, and thus, he was always making us think about basketball instead of just playing it. Coach Meyer truly has a learning program, and as players we were constantly forced to take notes and study the game. As I mentioned earlier, we were required to take notes in a 2" thick notebook that was handed out to each player and coach at the beginning of the season. But we did a lot more than just take notes.

Coach Meyer would also bring us articles, inspirational papers, or thoughts from other coaches and players in the profession periodically throughout the year. Piece by piece, our notebook would begin to fill with all types of information on the game from motivational topics, to articles on shooting form, to papers discussing playing as a team. Coach Meyer would never give us too much information at once; just enough for us to read at the end of a meeting or practice. Then, a couple of days later, he would give us another piece of information, and this would happen throughout the entire year. Coach would also sometimes bring books to practice, buying copies of books for the whole team, including John Wooden's book, *Wooden: A Lifetime of Observations and Reflections on and off the Court*, among others. I think Coach did this for two reasons. First, Coach Meyer simply loved the game of basketball and he loved to teach, and whenever he found any type of useful information about basketball he wanted to share it with his players, just as a teacher would share information with his or her class. Secondly,

Coach Meyer was giving us a huge competitive edge because we began to learn the game; not just play the game, but actually learn the game. By writing in our notebooks, reading articles from different experts of the game, and continually studying every aspect of the game we eventually would become a smart team. And, when two teams play that are equal in talent, we believed the winner would be the team that was smarter on the floor. We always wanted to be that team.

After Sundance finished his playing days, he was a graduate assistant under Coach Meyer and Coach had him write a quick article for the Wolves Newsletter that discussed the importance of taking notes in our program. Reading Sunny's article, he basically compared the basketball court to a classroom and a basketball player to a student. Basically, if a student wants to do well on a test, he or she will take notes and then review those notes before the test, right? Well, as a basketball player, the "test" is the game and also the practices that lead to the game, so before the game and the practices, the player / student should be taking notes to prepare for the "test." It seemed pretty logical to us as players, and it is something that Coach Meyer has done for many, many years with a lot of success. I know that once I have my own team, we (the players and coaches) will all have notebooks and continually take notes and study the game, because it is an area of the game that will give us a competitive advantage and will help lead a team to success.

Meeting Coach Wooden...

After the season ended, life went on as usual with school, our spring individual workouts and weightlifting sessions, and so on. Summer quickly approached, which meant another round of camps. While every summer of camps brought about different highlights and memories, this was a special summer because during the Coaching Academy the true legend of college basketball, John Wooden, was coming to Aberdeen, South Dakota to speak. As players, we all knew well in advance that Coach Wooden was coming to Aberdeen, and we couldn't wait. He was going to speak on the first night of the Coaching Academy, discussing his "Pyramid of Success" to the hundreds of high school and college coaches that were in attendance, and he was also going to be present the following morning for a "group photo" and what turned out to be a somewhat improvised autograph session. The Academy was going to begin with his speech at night, so before all of the coaches arrived us players had to help to get everything set up in the gym and in the auditorium where Coach Wooden was going to speak. We set up the concessions, the sign-in stations, the "soft goods" (which were shirts, shorts, etc.), and the video stations where Coach Meyer sold all of his tapes, and then a few of us found out that Coach Wooden had arrived and was going to do an interview with Coach Meyer for a local news station in a small classroom in the auditorium. I'm not even sure how some of us found out about it, but for those of us that did there was no way we could miss it. I can't remember which of the players actually snuck into the interview, but I do remember standing next to Houston Reed. We somehow got into the packed room full of cameramen and journalists right before it began, so we stood in the back and watched the show.

I can still see Coach Meyer helping Coach Wooden walk into that little room and setting him up in front of the microphones. At the time, Coach Wooden was just about ninety years old (it was in the summer of 2002), but we were all amazed at how sharp he still was. During the thirty minute Q&A session, Coach Wooden and Coach Meyer continued to joke with each other, just like two old friends that hadn't seen each other in awhile. It was amazing to watch. Houston and I kept looking

89

at each other, with a look saying "I can't believe we're watching this right now." It was amazing.

Later that night, Coach Wooden sat in a big, wooden chair in a dark auditorium in front of about four or five hundred coaches, talking for over an hour about how he created his "Pyramid of Success" and what each block in the pyramid meant to him. I had read about his pyramid in a couple of his books, but nothing could compare to him actually talking about the pyramid in person. It was so plain to see how genuine and serious he was about the pyramid. It took so many years for him to create the pyramid just the way that he wanted, and it was obvious that he believed with his whole heart every part of that pyramid (If you ever get a chance, buy one of his books and read about the "Pyramid of Success." It teaches much more than just basketball). Soon enough, his speech ended and it appeared that the night was over.

All of us players were hanging around the auditorium when Coach Meyer came up to us and told us to meet him at his house, that Coach Wooden was going to be there and that we would be able to visit with him for awhile, at least until he became tired. Obviously, we were all really excited. Not many people get the opportunity to visit with Coach Wooden on a personal level. We all headed out to Coach Meyer's house, and after about a half-hour wait he showed up with his daughter and Coach Meyer. The only people that were at Coach Meyer's house were the players, our coaches, and a few other people, including my Dad, who was a high school coach and a big, big fan of Coach Wooden.

When Coach Wooden walked in the house everybody was nervous and not really sure what to do as Coach Meyer helped him sit down at a small wooden table. Soon enough, we players all gathered around the table, and within minutes all eyes were on Coach Wooden. Every now and then one of us would have the courage to ask Coach Wooden a question, and he always had an amazing answer. I've heard a lot of people say how incredible it is to hear Coach Wooden speak because he is still so sharp and witty, and it's true. He answered all of our questions, throwing in jokes and poetry along the way. We could have sat in that room all night long listening to Coach Wooden speak, but soon enough the night had to end, and when Coach Meyer let it be known that Coach Wooden was probably getting tired, we all had to leave. Before leaving, Coach Wooden graciously signed a bunch of copies of his "Pyramid of Success" and took pictures with all of us players. It was easily one of the best experiences of my life. Once we left, I think everybody that was walking outside was in shock a little bit, because it was pretty silent. We were all just starting to comprehend how lucky we were to be able to sit and talk with a guy like Coach Wooden. It was truly an amazing night, and something that I will never forget.

Knowing how to "push a player's buttons"...

Before summer camp ended, I was feeling pretty good about myself. I was a starter during the previous season and had led the league in assists, and we had won our first league title since I had been a part of the program. I believe that Coach Meyer would say that I was beginning to feel a little bit too "comfortable." And the last thing that Coach Meyer wanted was "comfortable" players; he wanted "hungry" players; players that were always on the edge and never satisfied. So when he found the opportune time to challenge me during summer camp, he most certainly did.

As I've mentioned before, during our summer camps one of the highlights for the campers is to watch the Wolves players demonstrate the drills that they learn in during the night sessions that Coach Meyer directs. After the campers have worked on

91

their skills from 6 am to 9 pm, they get a much-deserved rest to watch the college players work out. It's a great experience for both the campers and the players because they get to see how intense a college workout should be, and they get to see how we handle Coach Meyer yelling at us.

I remember when Coach Meyer called me out, because it wasn't during the actual workout, but afterwards. Us players had just gone through about a half-hour workout, and Coach worked us hard. I probably had a pretty sloppy workout, either missing shots, demonstrating improper footwork, or just showing a negative body language, but whatever it was, I just didn't have a good workout. Coach Meyer undoubtedly noticed but didn't say anything until after the workout was over. As we finished our workouts, we had to grab our notebooks and take notes with the campers as Coach Meyer continued to talk, and that is when he grilled me. Coach Meyer didn't yell or anything like that, but he let me know in front of the two-hundred campers or so that my workout was unacceptable. He said something like, "Steve, I think you're too satisfied. You're coasting, your workout was garbage, and you better start getting after it! I don't want satisfied players!" Was I embarrassed? Of course I was embarrassed. Coach Meyer called me out in front of all the campers, and he made me feel like I was the size of the smallest camper in the gym, about the size of a six-year old little boy. But he didn't care. He had to send a message, and he never had a problem with sending it. Even though I was embarrassed and upset, I was immediately hungry again. I knew that I never wanted Coach Meyer to question my hunger and desire again, so for the remainder of camp and then for the remainder of the summer, I worked as hard as I have ever worked to improve my game and prove to Coach that I was more hungry than I had ever been.

IN THEIR OWN WORDS

Rob Browne, David Lipscomb University, Senior in 1992

I, like every other guy who suited up for Coach, had moments when I wondered what in the world I had gotten myself into. For me, it started on the day I officially visited Lipscomb. Sitting in the Hall of Fame room at McQuiddy Gymnasium and signing my scholarship offer (by the way, the only time anything signed by me will ever appear in the Hall of Fame room), Coach Meyer turned to me with a straight and stern face and said, "You know Rob, we're not worried about you bringing shame on the program or not developing as a player or person while you are here. The thing we're most concerned about is you getting your hair stuck under one of the lawn mowers used to keep the campus grass cut. That could be ugly for all of us." Thick, bushy, red, Waltonesque hair had been a trademark of sorts up to this point of my life. Grooming it well had not. Not even a hint of humor came across the man's face as he said that. Should I laugh? Should I return the jab? Should I ignore him? Should I get a haircut? I wasn't sure really. Two months later, I showed up at summer camp with a crew cut. I had been knocked off balance by the comment and pretty much remained that way the rest of my days as Bison.

I have more stories to tell on and about Coach Meyer than most former players I think. One reason was I was a 5 year player and another reason was that I looked for them. Storytelling is a great way to impress truth upon people. The Great Teacher of all history was a storyteller. While Coach would never call himself the greatest anything, he did weave a five year story line into the tapestry of my life that continues to challenge, rebuke, bear fruit, and influence me many years later.

I was never a guy who Coach would ask to lunch or sit down and chat with during the day. We were never friends during my playing days. Being a guy who nearly everyone on campus liked, it was a constant source of curiosity to me why I could not connect with this man on a personal level. I am sure I never became the player he envisioned when he recruited me. Fortunately, a year before me a guy named Hutch became a Bison and, two years after I signed, a scraggly haired kid named Pierce came along. What Coach needed from me was never 30, 12, and 2. What Coach did get from me were constant eyes and ears. While I might have disappointed as a player, I think I lived up to the student part of the deal. I soaked up more wisdom, humor, and narrative than many I shared that locker room with. I'm no better than any of them. I just knew that what I was getting as a Bison would have far more effect on me down the road of life than between the lines and in front of the crowds 3 nights a week. If we were to be friends, that would have to wait.

As a man today who administers youth camps in other countries around the world, I still laugh inside each time I read off our camp rules. Picking up trash, treating others the way you want to be treated, saying please and thank you, and taking notes will always be a part of anything I do. Inside those rules though were a penchant for the details and a commitment to the little things that has served Coach and his players well for many years. Not lost on me, even to this day, is the truth that greatness is in the details. Coach taught me that and for that I am grateful.

On January 8, 2005, my dear father died after living with Alzheimer's for the previous ten years. Many wonderful notes and calls came from teammates (not former for we will always be teammates) around the country. One I'll keep forever and treasure always was from Coach. In part, it read, "you father did a great job raising at least one of his sons. If you need me, call me. I'm here. Love, Coach." My brother did not know what to do with that comment but it surprised me little that, as in the Hall of Fame room in 1987, the man handed me a compliment and a quandary all at the same time.

People who are not friends don't say things like "I'm here", "call me", or "I love you." For whatever reason 1987 to 1992 were not in the realm of friendship, but that time built a platform of mutual trust and respect that I and Coach now stand on as friends. To know him as Coach had its challenges. To know him as teacher has its rewards. To know him as friend is the biggest blessing of all.

Jarod Obering, Northern State University Player, Senior in 2005

A lot can be claimed by an individual, but how others react is directly determined by their level of faith. The strongest asset Coach Meyer has as a coach, a teacher, and a mentor: He is genuine. If you doubt him once you will never make the mistake twice, because he will prove it over and over again. His players notice it first from his actions on the floor and in the locker room. When confronting his players and challenging them, his intentions are never pseudo. He really wants to develop his players on the basketball floor, and it is easy for them to trust his knowledge of the game and heed his advice.

After players learn to trust Coach Meyer's knowledge of

95

basketball, they begin to understand that his coaching does not end there. Coach believes in meeting as a team after practice to discuss and take notes on what the TEAM is trying to accomplish. It is the best time to review practice and what was emphasized that particular day. When my precious time of working with him on a daily basis is over, this is the aspect of his coaching I will miss the most. This is when his players learn not of his basketball knowledge, but of his wisdom in life. Every day he shares bits of information and advice that he has collected from numerous sources over his coaching career. Most of it covers important areas in basketball, but all of it covers important areas in life. And he does not hand it out and assume you know *why* it is important. He takes the time to interpret it *with you* (notice: not *for you*) and shines light on the areas that apply especially to the TEAM and the current situation. In this process of teaching his "pupils", it is easy to see how truly genuine Coach is. Coach will get so passionate at times he begins to get teary eyed. When some people cry it is not a phenomenon, but when Coach Meyer sheds a tear, it is as if raw passion is leaving his body. You see his lip quiver and feel the emotion in his eyes. The last thing going through your mind is doubt. You know he cares deeply about what he does, and what he does is help you.

A lot of people may possess a vast knowledge of their specialty. Some may even go a bit further by helping and sharing with others what they know. But the truly great ones, whether it is coaches, teachers, businessmen, or most importantly parents, live the example they preach. I am sure Coach was a great person to begin with. But in coaching, "there can be no happiness if the things we believe in are different from the things we do." [1] It means so much to him to be able to reach his players and help them in life. In order to do this, he understands the necessity of providing an example. In order to maintain this model he has continually improved himself every year of coaching by "making each day his masterpiece." [2] Through Coach Meyer, time has certainly showed the value in applying this to one's life. [1] Freya Madeline Stark – Travel Writer (1893-1993) [2] John Wooden's quote

My fondest memories of being a part of one of Coach Meyer's TEAMS:

Prior to the 2004-2005 season, our team was fortunate to have a "retreat" at Kessler's lodge a few miles south of Aberdeen. This lodge appeared to have it all: numerous televisions throughout the enormous building (centered with a giant plasma big screen in the main room), a pool table, shuffle board, two huge grills, and an outdoor basketball hoop with Sport Court, a hot tub, and even a putting green. It sounds like this would be enough to keep twenty young men busy for a night. And it would have been, had we gotten to them earlier in the night.

As soon as darkness hit, our entire team (even with a few hesitant individuals) began playing Bloody Mary (simply the opposite of Hide and Seek). We had players running through corn fields, mud puddles, and even a few small trees. This went on for hours into the night. It was nearly one in the morning when we finally finished playing. This may have been the most fun activity we did, but it certainly was not the highlight.

The highlight of the weekend came the next afternoon, when our TEAM was planning to do some TEAM-building. But we never got that far. We did not even get past the introductions. The first thing we did was talk about where we came from, who our family was, and why we came to Northern State University. This is when Coach Meyer set the pace, as all leaders do. I am not sure if it just happened (he said one memory kept bringing up another and another), but Coach spoke for maybe twenty minutes about the above areas (it seemed like only a few minutes, but when he speaks one loses the ability to track time. It seems to stop, yet fly by at the same time). After Coach

97

finished, he single handedly deepened every young man's thoughts in the room. Subsequently, our introductions lasted nearly the entire afternoon, and there was rarely a dry face in the group. It gives me goose bumps every time I think about that weekend. When the afternoon was already over, our TEAM caravanned back to town. I know every guy in our group felt differently about our TEAM after that weekend. There was so much love and understanding in that room, I hope each one of our guys will be able to experience that feeling again in their future. We have Coach to thank for that particular experience, along with many others.

Richard Taylor, David Lipscomb University, Senior in 1987

Steve, let me first thank you for investing the time to write this book. The thought of writing a book on Coach is an overwhelming thought. While it is easy and fun to take jabs at the man, the truth is that he is a great man as well as a great coach. I truly expect your book will be excellent; however, the task of writing a book that appropriately unveils the greatness of the man will be a difficult task.

It's hard to know what to say about Coach, since there is so much that could be said. What makes the man exceptional is not the fact that he knows basketball and teaches basketball at a level that rivals any coach in any league, but the fact that he uses basketball to transform boys into exceptional men. Not a day goes by that I don't reflect on my days as a Bison. Whether it's "Doing the next right thing right", or "Arête," or "Execute the fundamentals of the game for the welfare of the team", or "Leave the locker room cleaner than we arrived", or any of the other 1,000 thoughts or phrases I can regurgitate in my sleep, I depend on the Bison Paradigm to guide me through my life.

Coach is about the pursuit of excellence on and off the court. He is about being a student. He is about service. He is about the journey. Most importantly, he is about Jesus.

Just as it is hard to describe the impact Coach has had on me, it is equally as hard to share only one or two memories. I remember my first interaction with Coach at McQuiddy Gym when he told me, "Richard, the first thing you need to do is to completely destroy your body and rebuild it." I remember hearing no less than 100 times my freshman year that my scholarship was a one year contract if I didn't start doing things better. I remember the ultimate sense of team that I felt my junior year as we won the National Championship. That team truly had a singleness of purpose. Every person knew their role, executed their role, and was only focused on the success of the team. That was Bob Ford's team. I'm especially proud that we not only won the tournament, but we also received the Sportsmanship Award for the week. Winning the right way was as important as winning. I also remember how Coach made Chuck Ross a significant member of our family. Chuck is the same age as Coach, mentally challenged, and the biggest sports/Bison fan I have ever been around. He thought of Coach as his brother and Coach included him in everything. I remember camp when Coach, several times a day, would put on a Disney character hat and ride his bicycle into the gym of the younger campers and tell jokes. Some were funny but most were not. It didn't matter, everyone was told to hit the floor and roll in laughter (By the way, he still occasionally emails me and requests jokes from my kids). I remember wrestling in the Basketball Office, pinning him to the floor, and asking whose body needs rebuilding now. I remember the wave of emotion that hit me when I finally realized my career was over and I was now an alumni. Who wants to be alumni! I guess the point is that there is very little that I have forgotten.

I selfishly wish that more people had the opportunity to

know Coach Meyer as a man and as a coach. He has established a new standard for the title of "Coach". It is who he is, not what he does and there is no doubt in my mind that he is the best at what he does.

Thanks Coach,
Richard Taylor
'83-'87 DLU

Andy Foster, Northern State University Player, Senior in 2002

A Player's Coach and a Coach's Coach
Before we get started everyone needs to know these 3 rules:

1. Everybody takes notes.
2. Everybody picks up trash.
3. And everyone will say; "Yes sir, no sir, yes maam, no maam, please and thank you."

Great men do great things. Coach Don Meyer is a great man who does great things. Everyday he works on giving his gift of knowing the game of basketball and player development away to anybody who will listen, and anybody who asks him. Coach Meyer takes pride in sharing his love and passion for the game of basketball and player development each and every day. It doesn't matter if you are a 7-year old putting up jump shots in the gym all by yourself, or a successful coach yourself who has been coaching for 20 or 30-plus years, Coach Meyer will go out of his way to help you become the best player, coach or person you can become.

Those who were and are lucky enough to be a member

of Coach's teams past and present know and understand his passion for the game, as well as his passion for developing good young men. He will never set you up for failure, he will maximize your talents, and praise you every chance you get. He is also quick to give you constructive criticism when the time is right.

I will never forget the timeouts with the blood shot eyes, intense voice going off with spit flying as much as the voice and from time to time the 5-man sitting on the outside chair getting a nice little Charlie horse in the leg before taking the floor when Coach was unhappy. Another good memory is the day the whole team was kicked out of practice after the first 15 minutes of practice went badly. "You guys got 15 seconds to get your butts off this floor before I start kicking every one of them... 15, 14, 13, 12, 11, 10,..." Thanks for the day off Coach. Really though, thanks for the lessons, on and off the floor Coach.

With Coach Meyer and his players it is more then just molding a good basketball player...its molding a good person, student, brother, father, or husband. Coach Meyer wants to see people succeed. And if he can play a role in their success he will do what ever he can.

Coach I don't know if a simple thanks is enough. I just hope that it is a step in the right direction.

Sincerely,
Andy Foster

Matt Hammer, Northern State University Player, Senior in 2006

Playing for Coach Meyer is something I wish everybody could get the chance to do. You learn so much about the game of basketball, but more importantly about life and being a servant to others. We all know that Coach has won a ton of games but that's not what I'm going to remember about him after my career is over. I'm going to remember his desire to get better everyday and the way he pushes his players to improve not just on the court, but off it as well.

Andy Blackston, David Lipscomb University, Senior in 1998

The Trade off

If you showed up at just the right time in the Holman House after chapel, Coach would be finishing his nap and heading to Captain D's. If you knew how to work it, you could get a free lunch. You had to carry the coupon bag but the fish was good. It was during these times you had the chance to get to know the man behind the whistle. It was fun to talk about basketball with him. The trade off was you had to spend the next half hour after lunch driving around looking at houses. He liked to tell you who lived in every house and what they did. He even knew how much some of them made. We would drive by one house that had a yard that was spectacular. He would always make some comment like "if our team played like that man kept his yard, we would be in business".

The Trips

My most memorable moment with Coach Meyer was during Christmas break of my freshman year. He would usually take a trip to see other teams practice. I jumped in the car with Mark Campbell, Wade Tomlinson, Jason Shelton, Joe Horowitz & Coach and off we went. The first stop was Knoxville to see the Lady Vols practice. It was by far the most intense of the trip. Then we drove all night to Chapel Hill. We sat in the Dean Dome and watched Coach Smith practice for over two hours. Then it was off to Durham, NC. Coach K brought a special chair out for Coach Meyer so he wouldn't have to sit in the bleachers. We got to sit in on a team meeting. It was quite an experience for a freshman in college. We drove all night to get back home. This was just the first of many trips I took with Coach. He knew I wanted to be a coach and took the time to make investments in my future. We went to Evansville to see Jim Crews, Kentucky to see Rick Pitino, & Indiana to see Bob Knight. Those were great times. It was his way of showing that he cared.

The Accident

I was involved in a terrible accident in the Fall of 2002. I remember how concerned Coach was for my welfare. Whether it was a phone call, handout, or a note, he wanted to make sure that I knew he was there. Those acts of love meant more to me that he will ever know.

Andy Blackston

2002-2003:
"CONFIDENCE COMES FROM DEMONSTRATED ABILITY" JUNIOR YEAR

Recruiting...

One of the most unique parts of our program is in how we recruit players. Our coaching staff is no different than those in other programs in terms of scouting players, talking to coaches, going to camps in the summer, etc. but at Northern, I felt that we did something that many programs don't do before they make the decision of offering a player a scholarship.

All of the players that are recruited to Northern are brought in on visits, usually during the season so they can watch us play and get the feel for the environment of playing at the Barnett Center. Coach Meyer wants these recruits to experience as much of our program as they possibly can in just a couple of days, so Coach Meyer has them come to our pre-game practice, he has them sit in the locker room when we meet, and then he brings them in after the game is over to visit with the players. Not only does Coach Meyer want the recruit to get a good understanding of what our program is about, he also wants us players to get a feel for the recruit. In those two days that the recruit is in town Coach Meyer wants us to be around the recruit as much as possible, so when the recruit leaves for home, we have a good feel for the recruit. So how is this different than most programs throughout the country? In our program, Coach Meyer asks for our honest opinion of the kid. What type of a kid is he? Is he too cocky? Does he have values? Coach Meyer wants to know how we feel about the player, and there have been occasions where we have told Coach that we didn't like the kid. Maybe he was too cocky, maybe he was more concerned with other things than playing basketball, and we tell Coach Meyer. And, no matter how good that player is, if we didn't feel that he could fit in with the other players Coach Meyer would usually stop recruiting that player. Coach Meyer always believed that no player was more important than the program, regardless of his skill level. On the other hand, we (as players) had to be brutally honest with Coach so he knew how we really felt. The only way that this worked was that there was a great deal of trust and honesty in our program, and we knew that we could be honest with Coach Meyer and that he would be honest with us.

Coach B becomes a part of the program...

At the start of my junior season, we found out that for the first time the athletic department had hired a full-time strength coach. The coach's name was Derek Budig, a coach that had been one of the strength coaches at the University of Texas – El Paso, and had also worked with the Tampa Bay Buccaneers of the NFL, and we were all excited to see what Coach "B" would bring to the program. Well, he brought plenty. Over the next two years, he pushed us in the weight room, in conditioning drills, in plyometrics and flexibility drills, and in every aspect of being a college athlete that didn't deal with our actual playing on the court. Coach B instantly had a very close, trusting relationship with Coach Meyer and they worked together to setup the best game plan for the players during the fall, the regular season in the winter, and in the postseason. Coach Meyer gave Coach B full authority with our strength and conditioning program, and after about two weeks of training with Coach B we all knew he was the real deal. Coach B made us work harder in the weight room and in conditioning than we had ever worked before, but we willingly did it because of two reasons. First, we had guys on our team that were for the most part very self-driven and wanted to be the best, so we were willing to do what it took to get our bodies ready for the upcoming season. Second, it was impossible to not work hard for Coach B. He had more enthusiasm and energy than probably anybody that I have ever met. I don't know how he did it, but every time we met him in the weight room, on the basketball court, or outside on the football field, he was ready to go. We knew that we had to match his intensity or he would kill us, so we were also ready to go. Just watching Coach B for a couple of minutes was a sight to see. He was always interacting with the players, getting them juiced up for the workout ahead. I can still hear him saying, "Big Obie, we need one today. Get ready baby," and "Stevie, it's time to go, Stevie." "Let's go, Sunny, show these guys how to work big dog," and things like that. He was always barking out encouragement and instruction, jogging from guy to guy, bringing energy to the group. It was really amazing to watch.

It's hard to even describe some of the drills that Coach B made us do in terms of how difficult they were, but the key reason that we always came back ready to go is that he kept it fresh for us. Some days we would do conditioning in the pool, some days he would strap resistance cords around our waist and have us do sprints outside in the field, and some days we would do old-fashioned sprints on the hardwood. The secret was that we never knew what to expect. When we arrived for conditioning, we didn't know where we would be, but we knew that we were going to get a workout in wherever we were. The same applied to the weight room. Coach B created weeklong workout sheets for each guy on Sunday, and then we would go off of that sheet for the entire week. Each week, Coach B would incorporate different lifts and different reps to keep it fresh. That was the thing about Coach B. Just like all of his workouts, he was always fresh. He pushed our team to new levels and changed our bodies, making us stronger, quicker and more athletic, and ever since he has become a part of the Wolves family the program has reached new heights.

Energy Givers vs. Energy Drainers...

Something that I learned from Coach Meyer that I constantly think about when coaching or working in any type of group is his idea of energy givers vs. energy drainers. It's a simple enough concept, but one that has true meaning. On each team (group) there are going to be a number of different personalities some of which are outgoing and energetic, some of which are more laid-back, and some of which are very quiet most of the time. Regardless of the different personalities of the players on a team, each player is contributing in either a positive or negative way to the entire group. Coach Meyer made this point simple enough when he said: "As a player, you are always doing one of two things. You're either bringing energy to the team, or you're sucking energy away from the team. On our team, we want energy givers, guys that bring energy to the group." This is a simple enough concept, but Coach Meyer would constantly ask us what type of player we were on an individual level. Was I an energy giver or an energy drainer during the last practice? Did I make the team more energetic, or did I bring the team down? Constantly Coach Meyer would question every player on the team, and as my career progressed I began to see how important the concept was.

For anybody that has ever been a part of any type of group or team, or for a coach that has tried to "energize" a team, this concept applies. Whenever we become a part of a group it's pretty easy to determine within the first twenty minutes or so of a meeting what each person in the group is, whether it is an energy giver or an energy drainer. Some people bring energy to a group, whether it is through their talking or through their actions and other people drain energy from the group by their negative attitudes or their laziness. Coach Meyer knew that if we could get the majority of the guys on the team to be energy givers, the few remaining drainers would have to change their attitudes or get left behind. I truly believe that most successful teams and groups, in any type of business or sport, have at least an overwhelming majority of their players in the energy giver role (if not everybody on the team). At Northern, Coach Meyer wouldn't tolerate a guy that was sucking energy off the team, and Coach would always force the player to eventually choose between the welfare of the team or his (the player's) own selfish motives. More times than not that player would eventually buy into the team concept and bring energy to the team, benefiting everybody involved. One of the reasons we were so successful during my years, and why Coach Meyer is successful every year, is because he finds players that want to bring energy to the group. In Coach Mike Krzyzewski's book, *Leading with the Heart*, he says something like this: "Two are better than one, as long as two act like one. Imagine the power of five acting as one." That is what being an energy giver is all about; everybody on the team bringing energy to the team so that the team is in harmony, acting as one. It's amazing what a team can accomplish when everybody brings as much energy as possible to the overall goal of the team. Unbelievable things happen.

Let the Games Begin...

Finally, after a brutal preseason conditioning, lifting weights, and working on our skills, it was time to go. As a team, we were excited to say the least. Even though we had lost four seniors, including the conference MVP, both of our post players, and two starters, we felt that we were going to have a great season. We had three returning starters (I was at the point guard position, Nick Schroeder was our small forward, and Sundance Wicks was our power forward), a sophomore (Jarod Obering), that was going to be a great player as a shooting guard, and a ton of experienced returning players and three great freshmen recruits that were competing for playing time. After finally tasting a little piece of success in the previous season, we were all hungry for more. It was time for the season to begin.

We began our season with two exhibition games, first winning a home game against an all-star team composed of former college players called Howard Pulley (Minneapolis, MN) and then we traveled to Boulder, Colorado for our other exhibition game to take on the University of Colorado Golden Buffaloes, from the Big 12 Conference (Division I). The Buffs handed us a 91-70 loss, but we competed hard and learned a lot of things about our team before the real games began. Our first preseason game of the year was against a small NAIA school, Huron University, and we won easily by a score of 83-69. We followed that up by another game against an NAIA opponent, the University of Sioux Falls, a game that was to be played in Aberdeen on our home floor.

We knew that Sioux Falls had a lot of potential and that it was going to be a tough game, but we still came out flat. We couldn't really separate ourselves throughout the entire game, and they continued to chip away at our small lead. Near the end of the game, we were leading 70-69 when one of their players made a jump shot with 38 seconds remaining, as they took the lead for the first time in the second half at 71-70. We called a timeout and drew up a play, but as time was winding down we didn't get the look we wanted so I drove down the lane, taking a tough shot and missing it at the buzzer. We had just been beaten by an NAIA team for only the second time in the fours year that I had been a part of the program. We were all really disappointed in the locker room after the game. We knew that in our league it was very tough to get respect on a regional and national level once tournament time came around, and to lose to a team from a lower division was not going to help our cause. But, it was still only the second game of the season, and there was plenty of basketball to be played.

After the Sioux Falls loss, we rebounded nicely, beating Dakota State 98-62 and then pulling out a huge victory over a rival school from the North Central Conference, North Dakota State University in double overtime, 88-85. We were 3-1, and right in the middle of a five-game swing against teams from the NCC. We traveled to Sioux Falls, SD next to take on Augustana College, and after leading for the majority of the game, we let the Vikings crawl back into contention, forcing overtime. We were beaten in overtime, losing by a score of 76-70. We followed that game up with another road game against a very good University of South Dakota squad. For the third straight game, it took the extra overtime period to decide the winner, and we again ended up falling short 95-87. We then traveled to Grand Forks, ND to play another NCC power, the University of North Dakota. We lead for the majority of the game, but UND came back and hit a couple of huge shots down the stretch. We had plenty of opportunities to win the game, but we came up short, losing another heartbreaker by a score of 73-70. We had one more game before the Christmas break, a home game (finally) against one of our biggest rivals, South Dakota State. We hadn't beaten South Dakota State since I had been a part of the program, and we really wanted to get a big victory against them heading into the break. Again, we took a lead into our locker room at halftime and continued to play well in the second half, but as time was winding down they made the big plays and we didn't, and we eventually lost 73-69. We were all so frustrated. We had lost four straight games, and our record had gone from 3-1 to 3-5 in a matter of ten days.

After the game, Sundance was on the verge of tears in the locker room because he had never beaten our rival SDSU, and he knew that he probably would never get another chance because he was a senior. It killed me to see him like that, but it made me feel good to be his teammate, because the game meant so much to him. He had done everything he could on the floor, scoring 14 points and pulling down an impressive 14 rebounds, but we still lost and he took it the hardest. At that point, I realized that I only had a few games left with him and our other senior, Nick Schroeder, and I wanted to do everything I could to better our season. These guys were like brothers to me, and I knew that once our season (and their career) was over it was going to be tough to handle, so I wanted to try as hard as I could to lengthen our season for as long as possible. And I can guarantee that every other player in that locker room, watching Sunny cry and seeing the disappointed look on Nick's face, was thinking the exact same thing. Let's do this for Nick and Sunny.

Coming back from Christmas...

Once we returned back from Christmas, the conference season was upon us. We were currently sitting at 3-5 for the year, but we were confident that we would get things turned around. We started off the regular season with two games on the road, playing at Concordia-St. Paul (MN) and Winona State (MN).

We easily took care of Concordia, winning by a score of 78-60 and snapping our four-game losing streak. We felt that we had our confidence back as we traveled to Winona, MN to play a very good Winona St. team. The Winona game was a battle and an absolutely pitiful display of defense for both teams, as neither team could stop the other. We were down 85-83 with time running out when Sundance Wicks, who had made big shots for us all year, hit a floating jumper to tie the game at the buzzer and send it into overtime. We had the momentum and thought that we could get the victory, but in overtime, we still couldn't guard anybody, eventually losing 103-97, dropping our record to 4-6, 1-1 in the NSIC.

Some Players Have Heart, Some Don't…

During every season, different story lines always emerge. Some players that hadn't played a lot during the previous season become major contributors, and some players struggle to crack into the rotation. During my junior season, we had two such players that were both struggling to get minutes and whom Coach Meyer was particularly tough on. One of the players was Dell Mims, a junior college transfer who was extremely athletic and talented, but struggled to fit into the system and learn how Coach Meyer was expecting him to play. The other player, whom I won't mention by name, was having the same struggles trying to get minutes, and Coach Meyer rode both of these guys every day in practice. The interesting thing was how they responded in their own ways. Dell, whom we all expected to play a lot, continued to work hard in practice even though we all knew how frustrated he was that he wasn't seeing any minutes during the game. We could all see how frustrated and disappointed that he was, but the point is that he never gave up when Coach Meyer was really tough on him during practices. The other player basically just threw in the towel. Early in the year this guy was seeing a lot of minutes, but as his minutes deteriorated and Coach Meyer continued to be tough on him, he just gave up. He was non-responsive in practice and his actions in practices were to the point of being defiant, becoming a major distraction to the entire team.

The point is that Dell had heart, and this other player simply didn't. They had the same type of circumstances. Coach Meyer was equally hard on both of them, and in addition, he was harder on those two than on any other player on the team that year. Neither of these two guys were seeing any playing time (which can be devastating for an athlete in any sport and at any level), and both were frustrated. The difference is in how they reacted. Dell continued to "plug away" and try to get better, while the other player just gave up, biding his time until the end of the season, when he eventually transferred to a small NAIA school for his senior season. Dell came back for his senior season, and still didn't see much playing time throughout the year, but he continued to learn the game from Coach Meyer and improve his skills, and after he graduated he was selected to play on an elite traveling team called the Harlem Ambassadors, and travel all over the country as a professional basketball player. I am thoroughly convinced that if Coach Meyer hadn't been as tough as he was on Dell and if Dell hadn't stuck with the program and Coach Meyer's teachings, he never would have had a shot to continue playing after his college days were over.

My Shot...

As my junior year progressed, an interesting thing happened to me personally. While I was never a great shooter, I felt that I was always a guy that could hit the open shot when I needed to, but as my career progressed Coach Meyer made it clear that

113

he didn't want me to shoot a lot of three-pointers. During my junior year, I continued to shoot less and less, especially from the three-point line, and by the end of my junior year I had only attempted a total of ten three-pointers for the entire season (during my senior year I dropped the idea for good, shooting zero three-pointers for my whole senior season).

First of all, I'll go to my grave believing that I can still hit shots, and the interesting thing about the whole situation was that I started off my career primarily as a three-point shooter. In fact, during my freshmen season, 60% of my total shots taken (38 of 64) were from three-point territory, and my shooting percentage for three-pointers was 40%, which is usually considered very good. During my sophomore year my percentage dropped, and I think Coach Meyer started to believe that I wasn't a good shooter so he continued to discourage my shooting the three-pointer. And then I shot less as a junior, and didn't even attempt a three-pointer during my senior season.

As my career progressed, my not taking three-pointers became a doubled edged sword for our team. It was a bad thing because opposing teams that scouted us and looked at our stats knew that I wasn't going to shoot, so they played off me at least three or four feet which made it more difficult for me to penetrate (which was my strength), and it allowed my defender to clog the lane and disrupt our motion offense. It was a good thing, however, because by me not taking three-pointers and finding the guys on our team that were much better shooters than I was, our team was in a better position to win games. Coach Meyer believed (and he was obviously right) that for our team to have the best chance to win, the guys that were the best distributors of the basketball needed to do the distributing, and the guys that were the best shooters needed to do the shooting. So many other coaches that I've seen don't have the courage to tell some of their guys that they aren't good shooters and probably shouldn't be taking a lot of shots. Watching games at all levels today, I see so many bad shooters taking bad shots and hurting their team, obviously not getting reprimanded by the coach. The purpose of the game is to win, and I believe, just like Coach Meyer, that a team should do whatever is necessary even if that means that some players don't shoot a lot or in some cases, not at all.

Redefining my role: "D&D"…

I was at a crossroads. Teams were starting to play off of me four or five feet on offense and I basically wasn't allowed to shoot the ball whether I wanted to or not, so I had to find other ways to contribute to the team. I always knew what Coach Meyer expected from me on the floor, but I think when I finally realized how to perform my role was when I was no longer allowed to shoot. I knew that if I wasn't going to be a scorer, I had to be a contributor to the team in other ways and I decided that I had to do everything else as a player as well as possible if I was going to help the team succeed and if I was going to continue to get the minutes that I had been playing in the past. This is when I created the concept of "D&D." D&D stood for Defending & Distributing. That was my role on the team. Everything that I did as a player, every way that I could help the team had to come from being the best defender that I could possibly be and the best distributor of the ball to our other players that I could possibly be. As time passed I became a better and better defender, eventually having the role of guarding the best player on the opposing team (and more times than not, successfully taking that player out of the game), and I learned how to really play the point guard position on the offensive side, learning how to get our players the ball in a position where they were most likely to score. In fact, I wasn't even upset that I didn't shoot the ball; instead I came to take a huge amount of pride in

115

shutting down good players and getting our players the ball on offense where they needed it. "D&D" was the role that Coach pushed me to create, and once I learned what it was all about, there was no turning back.

Taking joy in doing the little things...

I wasn't the only player learning my role. Every player on our team was starting to "figure it out," as Coach Meyer would always say. At this point in the season, we were still struggling with a record of 4-6, but we were working hard in practice, and we were starting to really come together as a team. The older guys were starting to teach the younger guys what our program was all about and everybody began to understand what their role on the team was supposed to be. We started to know who was supposed to get the majority of our outside shots, who was supposed to initiate the offense, which players were supposed to do the majority of the screening, and which players we wanted to have the ball late in the game. Our team was beginning to come together. All of us players finally became willing to lose ourselves in the group for the welfare of the team, and at that point, we started to roll.

Rolling through the NSIC...

After we split games during the opening weekend of conference play, we came home to play a couple of games. We ended beating Wayne State (NE) handily by a score of 69-55 on Friday night and then winning again on Saturday night against Southwest State (MN) 67-60. We went back on the road the following weekend, beating Moorhead (MN) in a battle, 75-71, and then taking care of Minnesota-Crookston 75-44.

We had moved our record to 8-6, 5-1 in conference. The next weekend we were to play two of our toughest opponents at home, Minnesota-Duluth and Bemidji State (MN).

On Friday night against Duluth, we held the lead from the opening tip until six minutes were left in the game, when Duluth finally took their first lead, 56-55. The lead continued to switch hands until Duluth was up 64-62 with only thirty seconds remaining and the ball. We fouled and they converted both free throws to bring their lead to 66-62. We came down and Sundance shot a three-pointer, nailing it and bringing us to within one point at 66-65 with eight seconds remaining. Our crowd of 4,000+ was going crazy as it was apparent that another Northern-Duluth battle was going to go down to the wire. We immediately fouled, and they made one of two free throws, increasing the lead to 67-65 with seven seconds remaining. We called a timeout and Coach Meyer set up a final play where I was to drive the ball and Sunny was to "crack back," coming back to me for a hand-off and hopefully an open shot. We came out of the timeout and as the ball was in-bounded, I rushed down the floor, driving it and finding Sunny coming back to the ball. He took one dribble, and pulled up for three, shooting as time expired. It seemed as though our crowd was silent as the ball approached the rim, but as the horn sounded the ball clanged off the rim. Game over. Wait, wait, hold on. A whistle had blown, and after the chaos was sorted out, the ref called a foul on the shot meaning that Sunny was going to the line for three free throws and a chance to win the game.

First free throw: GOOD. Second free throw: GOOD. Third free throw: IN AND OUT. Sunny dropped two of three free throws, knotting the score at 67-67 and sending the game to overtime. Of course we wanted all three of those shots to go in, but we were all excited that we had a new life. There was now five minutes to determine the winner, playing in overtime for the fifth time of the season. We came out on a mission,

117

hitting big shots and getting stops on the defensive end, and Nick Schroeder finished the game by hitting four huge free throws as we somehow pulled off the victory, 79-75. It was a physically and mentally exhausting game, and even though we were excited we knew that we had another tough test the following night against Bemidji.

We came out flat the next night, and we could never create separation between ourselves and Bemidji. They were a very quick, athletic team and they gave us fits all night, forcing 19 turnovers and taking us out of our game. We kept it close throughout, but as the final buzzer sounded, we had lost 82-77, dropping our record to 9-7, 6-2 in conference. The next week we took care of Minnesota – Morris by a score of 82-62, and then we had two more home games the following week, winning a huge game against Winona State (a team that had beaten us earlier in the year) by the final 72-70, and then beating Concordia – St. Paul the following night 93-84. Our record had jumped to 12-7, 9-2 in conference. We continued to roll the following week, winning at Southwest State (MN) 73-61, and then going to Wayne State (NE) and winning a close one, 76-73. At home the following week, we took care of Crookston 77-56 and Moorhead 91-71, bringing our record to 16-7, 13-2. We had one final tough weekend ahead of us, going to Bemidji State, followed by another tough game at Duluth.

Round two against Bemidji was another close contest, and by the half, the Beavers had opened up a nine-point lead. We continued to claw back, but after another run midway through the second half, Bemidji was leading 63-50 and in control of the game. We continued to fight the rest of the game, and after making a run of our own we took the lead at 68-67 with less than a minute to go. Bemidji set up a play for their star center, Charles Hanks, and with nine seconds left he hit a tough shot and they recaptured the lead at 69-68. Instead of calling a timeout we pushed the ball up the floor and one of our freshmen players,

Adam Grant, took control and drove to the basket, shooting a tough shot at the buzzer. It "rimmed out" and we lost, 69-68. There was no time for feeling sorry, however, because the following night we had Duluth at Duluth, in a game we needed to win if we were going to capture the league title. We played well (as did Duluth), in a physical game that went back and forth throughout. As time was winding down another one of our freshmen, Aaron Busack, hit two free throws to clinch the win, 89-85. With a league record of 14-3 and only one game remaining we had clinched our league title for the second year in a row (the next closest team had five losses). We finished out the regular season beating a non-conference foe, Morningside, easily by a score of 100-75 and then we beat Minnesota-Morris 70-51 to finish the regular season at 19-8 (15-3 in league), to become league champions of the Northern Sun.

Wanting More...

The previous year, I think that we were really happy to get a piece of the league title, and while we weren't satisfied by just winning the league title, we might have felt that even if we didn't win the league tournament we still had a very successful season. This season was different, though. We had ran through the league finishing with a record of 15-3 (the next best record was 13-5), and we felt that we were the best team in the league. Therefore, nothing less than winning our first league tournament championship and moving on to the national tournament was going to satisfy us. That was our mentality going into the tournament.

It's a one-game season...

I remember talking to my dad before the start of the tournament and he mentioned something really interesting that I had never really thought about it. We were talking about the two seniors on the team, Nick Schroeder and Sundance Wicks, and how their careers had now been magnified into a "one-game season." He said something else, though, that really stuck in my mind. He said; "Nick and Sunny are living on borrowed time now." Living on borrowed time meant that these guys were basically done. All of the work that they had put into their collegiate careers, all of the practices, the games, the meetings, the lifting, conditioning, everything was almost over. At any point now, with a loss, their careers would be over. And because there was so much uncertainty as to when that loss would occur (would it be tomorrow, in the semifinals, maybe in the regional, or maybe in the national tournament?), they were in effect living on borrowed time. There was no more certainty left in their careers, there was no more control. All they could do (along with everybody on our team) was attempt to stretch the season for as long as possible.

The Conference Tournament...

Because we had won the league title we received the #1 seed in the tournament and we were to face the #8 seed, Concordia – St. Paul in the first round at home (the first round was always played at the home of the higher seed, and the semis and finals were played in Minneapolis, MN). We played a great game, hammering "the Golden Bears" by the final score of 99-65, advancing to the semifinals in Minneapolis for a third game against Minnesota-Duluth. Even though we had swept the season series with Duluth we knew how good they were, and we also knew that one of the most difficult things to do in sports is to beat a good team three times in a season. Surely, it was going to be a tough game.

I felt that our preparation going into the game was excellent. We were all a little nervous because we had still never won a tournament game in Minneapolis, losing in the semis the previous year and losing in the first round the two years prior, but Coach Meyer did a good job of convincing us that this was just another game and we prepared accordingly. Coach Meyer felt that we had to always stay on an even-keel and never play off of adrenaline or emotional peaks, because as John Wooden used to say; "for every artificial peak, there will be a corresponding artificial valley, and teams lose games in valleys." Therefore, our preparation for the game was the exact same as it had been throughout the entire season and we went into the game confident, knowing that we were the team that had swept the season series, not them.

Once the game finally began (our game was the second of four games played, sandwiched in-between the two girls' games), we couldn't wait. The gym was packed with nearly 3,000 people, which is about all that gym could handle, and it was loud from the start. From the opening tip, the game was a defensive battle. Neither team could find a shooting touch and both teams were playing hard-nosed, aggressive defense, and at the halftime the score was 33-30 in favor of Duluth. We opened up the second half on a 10-0 run, taking a solid 40-33 lead, and we extended our lead to eight points with only eight minutes remaining. At that point, I felt that we were finally relaxing, playing our style of basketball, and I had the feeling that we were going to finally separate ourselves from Duluth. I was wrong. Duluth stormed back with a 9-1 run, tying the game at 51-51 all with less than three minutes to go. Aaron Busack, our sophomore post, scored on a three-point play

121

to increase our lead to 54-51 and we had a chance to extend the lead but we uncharacteristically turned the ball over three straight times and Duluth capitalized, taking the lead at 55-54. After hitting two free throws, Duluth extended the lead to 57-54, and as time was winding down we had to foul. With less than ten seconds remaining they had a chance to finish the game, but their player missed the front end of a one-and-one and we rebounded the ball. Jarod Obering took the ball the length of the court, finding Sunny with time winding down. Sunny knew how much time he had to work with, and as he caught the ball outside of the three-point line, he faked once, took a dribble to his right, and pulled up for three with 0.7 seconds remaining. I didn't even know if he got the shot off on time because I heard the horn as he released the ball, but as he shot it, I felt confident he was going to hit the shot. Slowly the ball moved near the hoop, and as everybody in the gym fixed their attention on the rim, I saw the ball going through the net. SWISH! It was good! Sunny nailed the miracle shot with less than a second remaining, sending the game into overtime and keeping our season alive.

The gym was going crazy, as most of the fans were from Northern, and I was sure that we had the game in the bag at that point. Duluth was stunned that the game wasn't over (as I'm sure that we all were), and I felt that we could seize the momentum and grab the victory. As overtime started though, it was clear that Duluth wasn't going to just roll over. They had been in plenty of tough games, and they continued to fight. The score bounced back and forth for awhile but we could never get a good look (in fact, we didn't even make a shot in overtime; all of our points were from the free throw line). Duluth hit some big shots and we missed ours, and as time was winding down Duluth made their free throws, finishing the game with a 68-65 win. We had lost, and now our season was probably over. In the locker room after the game not many people were shedding tears because Coach Meyer let us know that we still had a good chance of making it to the national tournament with an at-large bid. Our record was good at 20-9, and usually teams that win twenty games make it into the regional, so there was still a chance. We had to wait until the tournaments in our region were over, and then wait to see if the selection committee felt that we deserved to make it into the tournament. Our destiny was no longer in our hands.

How the season ended...

Our locker room was a strange place after we lost the game because there was so much uncertainty surrounding our future. Was our season over, or would we get an at-large bid to the national tournament? Nobody knew for sure. Coach Meyer talked to us after the game, saying that nothing was certain but that he felt personally that we would get the invite. As players, that's all we really had to believe, so we believed deep down that our season wasn't over just yet. When we arrived back in Aberdeen we found out that the selection show for the Division II National Tournament was going to be broadcasted over the Internet on Monday afternoon, so we all met in Coach Meyer's cramped office, all fifteen of us, waiting for the show to begin.

Waiting for the selection show was about the worst feeling in the world. I had always watched the Division I Selection Show on ESPN, watching some teams explode with joy when they see that they made the tournament, but seeing other teams destroyed when their team doesn't appear on the final bracket. Sitting in Coach Meyer's office, we knew that in a matter of seconds we were going to feel one of those two emotions; we just didn't know which one it would be. Soon enough the show began, with each region being shown one at a time, slowly but surely. Finally, the North Central Region popped up on the computer screen, and we all stared, hoping to see Northern State University. It never happened. After finishing the year with a record of 20-9 we had not been selected, while a team from another league in our region was selected with a record of 18-11 ahead of us. We were all destroyed. The season was over, and we would never get a chance to play with this unique group of guys again.

The toughest part about the season ending was that we never really had closure. Usually in the locker room after the final loss, we all cry and reflect with each other, "closing" the season. But, because of the fact that we felt our season wasn't over when we lost in the conference tournament, we never had the closure in the locker room that we were used to. So, when we found out that we weren't making the tournament, it was a very empty feeling. We all walked out of Coach Meyer's office, and nobody really spoke. Some guys just left immediately, some guys hung around the gym for awhile, but there wasn't the closure that was so important to finish the season. I was personally devastated because I knew that I would never get the chance to play with two of my best friends, Nick Schroeder and Sundance Wicks, again. After being together for four years, their careers were over, and it was definitely a tough day.

The Wolfdog Festival…

One of the best traditions that we have at Northern is "The Wolf-Dog Festival." The Wolf-Dog Festival is a special day in the spring where Coach Meyer hosts a barbeque at his house for all of the different people that contribute to our program. All of the members of the Wolves Club (people that donate to the program), the school faculty, our great fans and alumni, and of course us players, are invited for the feast and hundreds of people show up. Now, the only meal that is served is the infamous Wolf-Dog. A Wolf-Dog is basically a hot dog that is sold at all of the NSU sporting events, but it is much larger and because our mascot is the Wolves, it is called the "Wolf-Dog." Believe me when I say that the people don't show up for the fine dining experience.

The great thing about the Wolf-Dog festival is that it is a special event that brings together every member that helps out the basketball program. Coach Meyer makes sure to invite everybody that contributes to our program, and it's always nice to bring the players and the "outsiders" together. In so many programs the players are seen as untouchable, and they never interact with the people in the community. Coach Meyer made it a point in our program, however, to always interact with all of the people in the community and to treat everybody with respect, because us players were no better (or worse) than anybody in our community. It was a great night to visit with people we usually didn't have the opportunity to talk to, and it was a great event to bring the entire Wolves program together. Coach Meyer picked up the bill for the entire night, and the community was surely appreciative. I don't know of too many coaches that basically invite an entire city over for dinner, but Coach Meyer did, and that is just another way in which he differentiated our program and showed his true side. To him, basketball was much more than winning basketball games, it was about developing relationships and being a good person.

Summer camp...

As summer approached, I realized that this summer would be the last time that I would be able to do summer camps as a player. It was a loud reminder that I was going to have a lot of "lasts" during the coming months (my last preseason workouts,

125

last "first day of practice," last "first game of the year," etc.) and I realized that I had to make the most of my remaining time. During that summer of camps at Northern, there were so many amazing experiences that I'll never forget, and here are a few of them…

The first experience dealt with Sundance headlining all of our camps. Over the past couple of years, Coach Meyer had picked up on Sunny's amazing ability to run camps, and as time progressed, he continued to give Sunny increasing responsibility and authority. By the summer of 2003, with Sundance having already completed his eligibility, Coach Meyer had pretty much given Sunny the reigns to run the entire camp. And Sunny did an amazing job running camps. First, Sunny had more energy than any other human being that I have ever met, so when all of the other players were beginning to drain as camp wore on, Sunny was still fresh. Secondly, Sunny had the God-given talent to work well with players of all ages, changing his moods from serious or angry to playful and joking in an instance. When Sunny was running camps, the kids were always on their toes because they didn't know what to expect from him. Sunny could be chewing out the entire camp for not working hard enough, and then with the drop of a dime he was joking with all of the kids, relaxing the mood. It's a talent that not many people have, but Sunny surely does. Finally, Sunny was both extremely organized and extremely passionate about running the camps. The campers could see how much he cared about making them better players, and they responded with their best efforts (that is why he will undoubtedly be a great coach in the coming years). He also could teach the game, because of his organizational skills. He knew exactly what he wanted to teach, and how he was going to teach it. He taught the game to the kids in a very simple manner, and they responded throughout their camp time to become better players.

Another one of the great memories that I have from the summer basketball camps of 2003 dealt with a local boy named Andy. Andy was a camp regular, a kid that we could count on to show up every year. He was a great kid, a kid that liked to have fun, and a hard worker. I had gotten to know Andy a little more personally because I had coached him during camp in a previous year and I also had refereed a lot of his YMCA flag football games in the fall, but that was the story with a lot of the kids in the area, so I didn't necessarily realize that Andy was any different than the others. I remember talking to Andy during a lunch break in our day camp that he was attending, talking to him and just joking with him like we always did with the campers. We were sitting there talking about Northern games, and how much he enjoyed coming to all of our games when he told me, "Coach Smiley, I bring a special nickel with me to every game for good luck because you're my favorite player." Let me explain. The number that I wore on my jersey was #5, and whenever we players would sign autographs for the kids, we all signed in a different, unique way. I would sign my name and then put a "5 cents" sign, instead of the #5, jokingly calling myself "The Nickel." Andy figured it out I guess, and so for every game, he would bring a nickel to the game as a good luck charm for me. When he told me that he did that for every game, I didn't even know what to say. I was so humbled and honored that a boy that I didn't even know that well would take such an interest in me. I realized at that point what type of an impact as players we have on people in the community. I guess that's why I get so mad to this day when players act like such idiots on television, in the pros or in college, in high school, and at all levels. Players don't realize that young kids look up to them and idolize them. I know that Andy's gesture made my day, and it made me realize again what being a college basketball player was all about.

Our last camp of the summer was called the Perimeter and

Post Play Positioning Camp, a camp that focused on the player's specific position. This was always one of my favorite camps to teach at because we were able to work with players that played the same position as we did. The Positioning Camp in the summer of 2003 was especially fun because of the size of the camp. Coach Meyer kept telling us as the summer progressed that the Position camp was going to be huge, but we didn't really understand until registration began and within a matter of hours, we had over 250 campers (the most campers that we ever had at a Northern camp at that point in time) jammed into Wachs Arena. As Coach Meyer gave his first speech of the camp, yelling at the campers to straighten up and take notes, the adrenaline was running. To see that many campers eager to learn the game and improve on their skills, us Northern players were just as excited as the campers to get started. For the next two and a half days we worked those campers extremely hard, teaching and pushing them to new heights, and when our short time together ended all of us Northern players felt that we had made a difference in improving their skills. It was a very rewarding feeling to have a successful camp with that many people, and it was a great way for me personally to finish my camp days as a Northern player.

An 82 Mile-Per-Hour Fastball...

At the end of the summer camp season, Coach Meyer always met with all of us players before the guys head for home for the final month or so before school starts. Coach Meyer would talk about how he felt we did in camp, and then he talked about what each player needed to do individually to make our team better. Even though most of the players were going home for the rest of the summer, Coach Meyer obviously expected them to be working on their individual skills and on improving their deficiencies to improve the overall team. Another thing that Coach Meyer usually did was find the players near the end of camp, usually on the last day, and talk to them in private about what they needed to do to make our team successful in the coming months.

I remember Coach Meyer finding me near the end of camp and I'll never forget what he told me. We were talking about what my role needed to be next year and what I needed to do to make our team successful. Coach told me that I had to be the leader on the team, that I was the point guard, and that I was a guy that the other players would respect if I accepted the leadership role. I had never been extremely vocal in the past, mainly because Sundance was so good at being a vocal leader, but with Sunny now graduated I had to step up and take control of the team from a vocal standpoint.

Then Coach Meyer talked to me about what I needed to do to continue to improve my game. I had just finished my second season as the league leader in assists, and I felt that I had had a pretty good year. Coach Meyer made sure that I continued to get better and better by telling me straightforward that I wasn't a naturally talented player. He said, "Steve, you have to go to work every day, working harder than the next guy, because you only have an 82 mile-per-hour fastball. You don't have a 95 mile-per-hour fastball, so you have to outwork the other guy." After starting for two straight seasons and being fairly successful, I needed Coach to tell me something like that. The last thing that I needed going into my senior year was Coach Meyer telling me how good of a year I had and how happy he was with me. No, I needed Coach to motivate me, to push me to greater heights. And Coach, knowing that I was a very self-motivated player and would try everything I could to prove him wrong, said exactly the right things to keep my blood boiling. I wasn't necessarily happy that he told me I was only an average player, but I was certainly motivated. The most

129

important thing about our talk though, was that Coach Meyer wasn't just talking about basketball; he was talking about life. He knew my personality, and as he had said before he felt that we were very similar, so he was preparing me for life and how hard I would have to work every day if I wanted to succeed. The funny thing is that to this day, whenever I'm tired or just feel like being lazy and taking the day off, I still hear those words; "You're only an 82 mile-per-hour fastball pitcher." And I become motivated all over again, working hard to prove Coach wrong.

IN THEIR OWN WORDS

Derik Budig, Strength and Conditioning Coach, Northern State University, 2002-present

I knew Coach Meyer was different within a month or so when I was hired as his Strength and Conditioning Coach. I think it must have been the countless times I would walk by his office and he would call me in; inevitably he would ask me if I read this book or that book. Coach, in the same sentence, would be writing in his planner and handing me a brand new book he wanted me to read. Talk about a multi-tasker, he should be the spokesman for it.

What impresses me more about Coach is his humble, servant attitude. It reminds me of the first chapter in *The Purpose Driven Life*, by Rick Warren. The opening chapter states, "It's not about me." Well, with Coach it's not about him, it's about the team and his ability to communicate and live it out each day. I can't tell you how many times I get a comment or an email saying Coach Meyer speaks highly of you (me). Coach always gives credit to everyone else but himself, which reflects the attitude of no one being bigger than the team!

Lastly – he is dedicated to Jesus Christ! In a world that says we should tolerate everyone and everything, Coach does not. He doesn't apologize for it either; in fact he embraces the opportunity to exploit Jesus for the sake of others. Coach often purchases bibles for his players and coaches, as well as handouts on different Christian perspectives on a daily basis. I think the biggest thing that I learned from Coach is the fact that being a Christian man doesn't make you soft and timid, but instead the Holy Spirit fills your soul with a love that is unconditional. No matter what I do or the players might do to disappoint him, he will always show you his love. That love may be in a form of discipline or calling you on the carpet with regards to your play or actions, but it is still his love that drives you to be a better person. I think I could talk about Coach for hours, he is such a unique man with unique qualities, but it will never be about Coach, it will always be about others.

Marcus Bodie, David Lipscomb University, Senior in 1990

There are so many great experiences that I have had playing under Coach Meyer. I think one of my favorites was on the first day I came up to Lipscomb, when Coach told me that he was going to turn me into a point guard. He gave me two basketballs and showed me some drills and said "All I want you to do this yeas is work on your ball handling skills." Of course in my mind I was thinking "Coach I need to learn how to shoot better since the 3-pointer had just been implemented into the game." It was about a 3-second thought. Puff!!

During the beginning of the season Coach was breaking down everybody's role on the team, the "what you can do and what you cannot do." Well, again one of my thoughts was that my strengths would include shooting. Wrong!! Coach told me that I was not going to be a shooter, but more of a ball handler and a defensive specialist. I took that recommendation in stride, and every now and when I got into the game I would take a shot. I thought these were good shots and Coach would still take me out. I got the point very quickly, so I was in a game during the middle of the season and I got a steal. It was just me, the ball, the basket, and the words of Coach Meyer: "You are not a shooter." So as I was going to lay the ball up, those words came into my mind and being the disciplined player that I am, and learning to follow directions, I dribbled around the goal and under the goal to the sideline where Coach Meyer was yelling "Shoot the Ball. Shoot the Ball. Why didn't you shoot the ball?" Dribbling close to the sideline, I said "Coach, you told me that I COULD NOT shoot the ball." He gave me that look of his.

After the game, we went into the locker room for the post game team meeting. Coach immediately redefined my role at that point. He said "From now on, Bodie can only shoot lay-ups and free throws." Well, as a freshman I accomplished one of my goals. I proved to the coaches, team, and myself that I could be a scorer, even if all I could shoot was lay-ups and free throws. I became a scorer over the years, and I slowly developed a shooting touch, even having some 20-point plus games. Coach knew how to slowly develop players into the players that we wanted to be. He had a vision for our talents even before we realized it. He turned me into a player that people still today respect and love. I have that same vision for the kids that I coach now. I understand why it had to start with me first: my attitude, my desire, and especially my will to learn. Coach Meyer is a great teacher who has the patience and tenacity to get the best out of his players. The things I have learned from him are embedded into my soul for eternity. Coach Meyer is a bonafide COACH: C-Caring; O-Overachiever; A-Arête; C-Christ-Like; H- Hair Less Humble. Thanks big guy!!

MARCUS BODIE

Brad Christenson, Assistant Coach, Northern State University

I really don't even know where to start. I can't even begin to tell you how fortunate I am to have had the opportunity to work with Coach Meyer. I only wish that everyone could get to know Coach the way that I do and see what I get to see on a daily basis. The basketball success that he has had as a coach is only part of what he is all about. If only people could see. . .

- The way he jokes around with people.
- The way he is around kids.
- The things he does for people that no one ever knows about.
- The way he teaches life through basketball.
- The way he pushes people to be the very best they can be.
- The time he puts in.
- The passion he has for teaching and for the team.

. . .

So often in life we don't appreciate what we have in our lives until it is too late. We also way too often don't tell someone how we feel about them or thank them for all they do. So Coach I want to tell you thanks for everything. I have loved every minute working with you. You are the best!

BC

Paul Sather, Northern State Assistant Coach
(with Coach Meyer 1999-2004)

It is difficult to find a coach that equals Coach Meyer in their passion for teaching the game of basketball. Fundamentals and team attitude are the building blocks for his basketball teams. That requires a great deal of commitment, not only from Coach Meyer, but also from his staff and the players. Only since I have taken a new position have I realized the total impact his program can have on a person. Coach Meyer most of all wants to help young people get ready for life after basketball, and he uses the game of basketball as a vehicle to do just that. What is most amazing about Coach Meyer is that of all of his accomplishments, none are as important to him as the success his former players, managers, and assistant coaches have had after being in his program. In a sport where graduation rates are always under criticism, coach has graduated all but two of his former players in the 30-plus years he has been coaching.

No one has more fun at what they do than Coach Meyer. Coach is an instigator by nature. Everyday he loves to set people up for some joke, to tell a joke, or to take a picture of someone with his water camera. You can count on him exploding with laughter at some point and time everyday in the office, and if you're standing next to him he'll catch you with that left-jab to the shoulder as to say, "That was a good one." He loves to laugh, no matter if he is laughing at himself or someone else (although he preferred laughing at someone else). Going to lunch has always been an important part of his day. In Nashville it was Captain D's, and in Aberdeen it is McDonald's (This could explain his quintuple by-pass surgery he had four years ago). He has a great loyalty to the people that give him the most food for the cheapest price. At Lipscomb they still used coupons from 1987 in the late 90's. One thing our new coaches would

135

learn right away when they joined our program was never to "super size" their meal, Coach would never let you forget it.

The other side of Coach Meyer is when he puts the whistle on. When it was time to practice, it was time to stop "jacking" around. Our practices were planned with great detail; fundamentals and competition were two important areas Coach stressed each day. Our practices were very demanding and there was not much time for rest. Coach never liked going longer than two hours. Individual skill development was the life-blood of our program because we didn't always have the most athletic players. We had to play harder, smarter and together to give ourselves a chance to have success. Coach spent time on shooting, passing and ball handling drills each day. Even if it was only for a few minutes…it was important. Coach Meyer looked to challenge our players both physically and mentally, making practices harder than the games. We really believed the work we put in gave us the advantage no matter who and where we played.

I will never again be a part of something like I was at Northern State and with Coach Meyer. He is one of the few people in this profession that truly lives up to the name, "Coach." Coach Meyer is the consummate teacher and is totally selfless when it comes to his team. I have been truly blessed to have had the opportunity to work with Coach, and his lessons have changed my life. He has helped me be a better coach, but more importantly, he has helped me become a better person.

Paul Sather – Northern State 1998-2004

Ricky Bowers, David Lipscomb University, Senior in 1996

Coach has become a Wolf in a far away territory but he continues with me as if he were still a Bison. There are few days that pass that I do not rely on his teachings. There is a consistent voice that asks me "what would the Guru (Billy Mooney's prescribed name for Coach) do"? I sleep less, work smarter, read more, say please and thank you often, obsess little things, study with greater desire, ask why, give more, compliment the weak, criticize the strong, run farther, laugh at myself and love more deeply because of Coach Meyer's lasting influence. He taught me the importance of teaching and coaching and inspired me to pursue this profession.

We have all read the hundreds of cards coach has handed us over the years. I am reminded of the one titled "Little Eyes Upon You." Coach gave us those cards to keep us aware of all the little guys in camp who would no doubt emulate our actions and words. Is it not amazing how many of us players became the "little fellows" who have become just like coach?

Philip Hutcheson, David Lipscomb University, Senior in 1990

It was my first year of Bison basketball camp. It was Coach Meyer's first year of Bison camps too when we first met. Far from the thousands of people his camps draw now, there were maybe 150 or so total, and every worker there, including Coach Meyer, coached two teams, refereed two games, started working early bird clinics at 6:00 am, and didn't quit until around midnight. I wore green running shoes, tube socks with three stripes pulled to my knees and big brown plastic glasses.

He wore sweats, a whistle and a scowl. I wasn't yet 10; he was in his mid-30s. Most basketball camps were about swimming, break time and playing 3 or 4 games a day. Coach's camps were about fundamentals, pushing yourself farther than you thought possible and learning that the most important lessons basketball taught were the ones that helped you more off the floor than on it. Although almost all I remember doing that week was push-ups, snake-rolls and "sitting on the wall," I loved the camp, and I went away wanting more.

It was my first paycheck I ever earned. $ 75.00 for a week's work at the concession stands of Bison Basketball Camp. While the average observer would have seen only a goofy kid bouncing around out on the court, Coach saw something else. That year, he let me work for him, and as he's done with thousands he's met in camps and clinics since, he taught by example how we're supposed to treat those who cannot do anything for us in return. Since then, countless are the times that I've seen Coach Meyer send a note, share a meal, give a ride, or in some other way make feel important a person to whom he owed nothing and from whom he expected nothing in return. In me, he took a young person who, at the time, certainly showed no signs of doing anything on the basketball court, other than injuring himself, and allowed him the first taste of what it's like to be a part of something that is bigger than any one person. Although it was only a few weeks, and most of my job involved mopping floors and serving cokes, I had experienced what it was like to be a part of a Coach Meyer "team," and I went away wanting more.

It was my first practice as a college basketball player. The season was only a couple of months away, and it was our first team meeting. Surely we'd get right into various offenses, defenses and out-of-bounds plays. Looking back at my team notebook (I still have all four years worth at my house today), the first day headings included, "Taking Responsibility," "Team

Attitude," and "Common Courtesy." Not a word about anything on the court. It didn't take me long to learn that for Coach Meyer, learning the fundamentals of the game in order to be a good player was important, but learning the fundamentals of life in order to be a good person was even more important. For every "block out" or "move your feet" I have written in those notebooks, I have just as many "do the next right thing right," "say please and thank you," and "leave a place better than you found it" written as well. Very few people demand greatness out of you, and fewer still will actually help you achieve it. Coach did both. Although we would (and still do) often kid Coach Meyer about the connections drawn in a single team meeting between, for instance, Dick Butkus, the habits of amorous Bengal tigers and help-side defense, somehow, he would end most meetings with a valuable life lesson, and invariably, I went away wanting more.

It was my first game as a college player. Two senior post players graduated off of the National Championship team from a year earlier, and I started in one of their places' with decidedly low expectations. Somehow, in that first game I scored over 30 points. After the game, Coach Meyer took me aside and told me that even though it was one good game, I still had miles to go as a player. As I was to learn in the years to come, for Coach Meyer, basketball and life are both about continual improvement. Albert Schweitzer once said, "I'd rather see a good sermon than hear one any day." Coach Meyer lives a good sermon. Whether it's secretly whispering into one of his Dicta-phones, scribbling a note on a Captain D's napkin or quizzing a local junior high coach about an in-bounds play, Coach Meyer was the type of coach who was constantly learning, who was constantly expanding his borders, and who was constantly demanding greatness of you. But Coach earned the right to do so by demanding greatness of himself as well. Although in my first game I had played a game that exceeded any I thought

139

I might have had in my college career, Coach quickly let me know that not only was improvement possible, but it would be expected the next day, and the next, and the next, and I went away wanting more.

It was my first hour after my career had ended. We had lost in the National Semi-Finals by two points. A reporter asked me about the disappointment I felt at that moment, and I told him that as strange as it sounded, the loss itself wasn't really what made me most sad. It was the ending of a special time with a special group of people that made me most sad. A time and a group where, thanks to Coach, everyone cared about the other person more than himself, where everyone was focused on a common goal, and where, to those who mattered most - to your teammates and coaches - the effort really did matter more than the outcome. Four years earlier Coach Meyer had planted the seeds, and it had taken four years of summer camps, early morning workouts, pre-season scrimmages, drill upon drills, endless team meetings, long bus rides and more for his lessons to fully take root. Although I was sad we did not win the National Championship, I was more saddened that such a special time with this special group Coach had built had come to an end. Even then, I knew what a rare gift I had been given- being a part of a real team - and I went away wanting more.

It was the first week after my teammate's son had died. Anyone can be a good teammate when you're all winning and laughing and having a good time. But almost 10 years later, as I sat on the porch of my friend's house, I thought of what a testimony it was to the bonds that Coach Meyer's program had created that so many of "the Bisons" had come back to rally around a teammate who was struggling. Many that came lived hundreds of miles away, and many of those were guys who didn't even play in the same years together. But they came just the same. They came just because "one of the Bisons" was in need. But that was to be expected. The last words that I wrote in my notebook that Coach said to us after our final loss my senior year were, "Being a Bison is still more important than winning or losing." And as Lipscomb University considered the move to Division I, Coach Meyer was struggling with a decision to stay or go as coach. If he were just another coach, he would have been back in Tennessee, talking to administrators and boosters, worried about his basketball program, and trying to help save his program. Instead, he was in Indiana, talking in front of a crowded church, worried about a former player and friend, and trying to help others who were hurting. He was there, and not in Nashville, because he wasn't and isn't just another coach. And although we all knew that nothing said was going to change the situation, Coach Meyer still encouraged us all that day with words that both comforted and inspired, and I went away wanting more.

It was the first time I talked with the Sports Information Department at Northern State University. They told me that Coach Meyer had just been hired as the new Head Coach, and they wondered what I would have to say. I told them that even though they didn't know it, Northern's players had just been enrolled in the best class they would ever take while in school. And although they will certainly learn many of the same lessons I did from Coach, when their time as a player is up, I'll bet they, like me, will all go away wanting more.

2003-2004:
"CLOSURE"
SENIOR YEAR

A Bad Start...

The start of my senior year (2003-2004) was definitely rocky. Before school had started, I took a couple weeks to go home to Denver to work out some details for my wedding that was going to take place the following summer. Most of the other guys on the team were home as well, taking the last couple of weeks to spend some time with their families and friends because once the school year started, it was difficult for most of the guys to get home at all, except for a quick break during Christmas. I remember on the road trip back to Aberdeen I received a call from Nick Schroeder, who was now one of the graduate assistants for the team. Nick had told me that a couple of the guys had been in trouble with alcohol, and to call him right when I got back to school.

It wasn't a huge deal in that the violations were fairly minor, but I think that it put a bad taste in Coach's mouth before the season even started. Before class had officially started, Coach Meyer called us all in for a meeting and he was not happy. Every person on the team was questioned about what was really important to them, and Coach made it clear that if there was any more trouble in the near future, the roof would come caving in.

Coach Questioning Our (My) Leadership...

During that meeting, one of Coach Meyer's overall "themes" was that he wasn't sure if we had the leadership on the team to have a good year. He wasn't sure if any of us would have what it takes to be the leader of the team. The previous year, Sunny was a senior and he was undoubtedly the team leader. Whenever anyone on the team had a problem, Sunny was the first guy the player would talk to and whenever the coaches needed a player's input, Sunny was that guy. With Sunny graduating, Coach Meyer was obviously concerned about our leadership.

Being that I was one of two seniors, and that I had started for the previous two seasons and was the point guard, Coach expected me to be the leader, and during that initial meeting, he singled me out and questioned my individual leadership responsibilities. One of his biggest worries was that I had "too much on my plate," being that I was getting ready to graduate in the spring, worrying about what I was going to do after college, worrying about the team and the upcoming season, and getting married two weeks after graduating, to top it all off.

Going into that senior season and knowing that it was my responsibility to be the leader, I knew that I couldn't be Sunny. He was very outgoing and vocal, and he was somebody that the guys had a very easy time talking to. I, on the other hand, knew that my leadership style had to be different than Sunny's, simply because I knew that I wasn't as vocal as he was and I knew that I would have to take a different approach to gain everybody's respect as a leader. Even though I knew that I did have a lot of things on my mind, I was ready to prove to Coach Meyer and the guys on the team that I could be a leader and help the team to a great season.

Group Huddle...

Going into the season, one thing that I wanted to try with the team was something that I learned from Coach Jerry Krause at Gonzaga University. The summer before my senior season, I went up to Spokane, Washington to work some camps at Gonzaga with three of our players (Nick Schroeder, Matt Hammer, and Taite Plaas). I was able to spend some time talking with Coach Krause, whom I knew before our trip because he is a very close friend and former coach of Coach Meyer's, and I asked Coach Krause if the Gonzaga players did anything special to prepare for games, practices, anything at all. He told me that before every one of their practices or games the whole team would get in a huddle without any coaches or managers, just the players, and they would take a minute to talk as a team and get ready for the practice. Coach Krause told me that he wasn't sure what they ever said in that huddle, but whatever it was, when they came out of it they were ready to go. Thinking about it, I loved the idea to gather before all team events with just the guys, and just completely get everybody focused on the task at hand.

At the very start of our preseason, I talked with a lot of our older guys about the huddle idea and everybody liked it, so we tried it out. Before every lifting session, and especially before every conditioning session, the whole team would circle up and every guy in the circle would have to commit to the task at hand, saying that they were ready to go. After everybody in the circle had given their personal commitment, we stacked up and said our trademark "Pride in the Pack" and it was time to work.

As the season rolled on, we didn't huddle before every practice because the guys would get to practice at different times and Coach was always working with players before practice officially began, but we did huddle before every game. We had a hallway in the Barnett Center that we would walk down before the start of the game, and as we reached the end of that hallway and could see the fans in Wachs Arena waiting for us to storm the court, we would all huddle up with every person committing to the task, and then it was time to go. When we broke that huddle we were all so jacked up that we really didn't know what was going on, but it was an amazing feeling to break the huddle and storm the floor. Being in that huddle right before the start of a huge game will be one of my favorite memories at Northern.

Struggling With New Changes in my Life...

As I mentioned earlier, I was going through a lot of things in my life at the start of my senior season. Looking back, I'm not sure how I was able to manage all the demands on my time and still be fairly successful and efficient in my life, except for the fact that I had learned to plan my days, weeks, and life priorities fairly well, something that Coach Meyer had taught me throughout the previous years. There were many times during my senior season that I did feel overwhelmed, but every time that I had that feeling I tried to just take a step back and think about all the wonderful things that were going on in my life. Sure I was busy, but I was also getting ready to graduate college, I was playing college basketball, and I was marrying a very special women. Sometimes, I just needed to look around me to realize how lucky I was to be so busy.

I think that having so many things "on my plate" really motivated me in every area of my life. It's funny how when a person seems like they are unbelievably busy they usually get the most done. I know that was, and still is the case for me. Anyways, at the start of the season a lot of people around the athletic building were jokingly giving me a hard time that I wasn't going to have a good year because I was getting married, and I just couldn't possibly have the right focus. Even though they were joking, those people actually motivated me to have my best year ever, just so I could prove that my marriage wasn't a distraction. There were times when I would get extremely mad when people would ask me if my fiancée Nikki was taking away from my basketball time because she was so laid back and she made sure that basketball was my first priority. If anything came up regarding our wedding during the season, she took care of it because she knew that I didn't need the stress. Nikki was my number one fan and she kept me sane through the season.

Preseason Conditioning...

In our program the most exciting, but also most dreaded time of the year has to be the fall. It was really exciting to get everybody back to start doing our individual workouts with Coach Meyer twice a week, scrimmaging at night, lifting four times a week, and just being back together as a team, but the one excruciating part about the preseason was the conditioning with our strength coach, Coach Budig. We conditioned twice a week with Coach "B," once on Wednesday morning at about 6:00 am, and once on Sunday afternoon, around 5:30 pm. Preseason only lasts for about six weeks, which means that we only had probably twelve sessions of conditioning, but believe me when I say that each year they were twelve of the hardest hour-long sessions that I have ever been through.

It seemed that on average, we had at least one guy vomit per session, and it was just because the sessions were that hard. Everybody on the team knew it was going to be a butt kicker, so we all drank plenty of fluids and ate healthy, but it didn't really matter for some guys. Tony Birmingham, one of our guards, puked almost every time during my senior season. He was in shape and ate really healthy, but for whatever reason he lost his lunch pretty much every time we stepped on the floor for conditioning. The majority of the time we did our conditioning in the gym and we would start with a lot of agility and plyometric work, but the last twenty minutes was what we all feared for. That was when the conditioning would take place. Coach B would definitely keep things fresh during conditioning, in that sometimes we would do station work, sometimes we would do full sprints the whole time, and sometimes we didn't have a clue what we were doing, but the only constant was that by the end of the day there was absolutely no gas left in our tank. Even though it was physically grueling to go through those sessions, every guy on our team knew that what we were doing would benefit us once the season started, and sure enough, when the first day of practice hit around October 15th of each year, we were already in great shape.

Great Start to Practice...

After the rocky start at the beginning of the year we really came together as a team and had a great preseason. Everybody worked hard and as a team our strength, stamina, and skill level all improved. When practice started on Ocotber 15th, we were rolling. Usually the most enthusiastic, energetic practice of the year is the very first one, because it's fresh and everybody is excited. When the season rolls on, however, things can become "stale" and the daily grinding of practice wears on almost everybody involved with the team. Our team was no different in that our first practice of that season was electrifying. Everybody was sharp, and we all felt like we accomplished a lot in a short amount of time. Coach warned us after that practice that it's   147 normal for everybody to be into it on the first day, but the test of a real team is how they practice on day 2, 3, 4, and so on. I think that everyone on the team took that speech to heart, and our first few weeks of practice were excellent.

Usually college teams, at least at the NCAA level, have about three weeks of practice before the exhibition games begin. Most teams play two exhibition games, and we were slated to play Division I teams Vanderbilt and Austin Peay, both located in Tennessee. I think everyone on the team wanted to show that we could compete with big-time Division I schools, and that kept our momentum up in practice. Going into our Tennessee trip, everybody was ready to go and everybody felt good about how far we had already come as a young team that was going to be playing a lot of freshmen and sophomores. Our learning curve during those first couple weeks of practice was huge, and we all felt that the season had started off in the right way.

Tennessee Trip…

It's always exciting for a Division II team to play exhibition games against Division I competition, because as players at a Division II school, we always wanted to know how we would stack up. With Coach Meyer having a lot of personal relationships with Division I coaches he was able to schedule at least one Division I game per year as an exhibition. Playing against that type of competition did nothing but benefit our team because we were always undersized and physically out-manned, so we had to rely on fundamentals and good teamwork to stay in those games. In addition, after playing schools in the SEC, Big 12, or other major conferences, we came back to the Division II level very confident of what we could do. Outside of playing the actual games, those exhibition trips were always a great experience and opportunity for team-building, and during my senior year it was especially important because we had so many new guys and it gave us the opportunity to spend almost a week on the road with just the guys; no family, girlfriends, or other distractions were present.

We left for Nashville early in the week on a chartered bus, and after staying midway somewhere in Missouri, we arrived two days before the game. Coach felt that since the season was still so early, we would have full practices both days prior to the game, because we needed the work and couldn't waste an opportunity to get better. After practicing for a couple days, we were ready to play Vanderbilt. Vanderbilt was picked preseason to finish fairly high in the SEC rankings, and they had the preseason player of the year, Matt Freije, so we knew it was going to be a difficult game. But, when the opening tip came, we played really well and at halftime we were only down three points, feeling that we could have gone into the locker room with the lead. The second half was a different story, as the Commodores ripped us apart from the opening bell. I'm assuming their coach gave them the wakeup call that they needed, and when the second half started, we were just absolutely inferior physically. We ended up losing 86-57, but it was a great experience (especially for the younger guys), to play against that level of competition. As a side note, Vanderbilt went on to make the NCAA tournament and go all the way to the Sweet 16 that year.

Our second exhibition game was against Austin Peay, a very talented mid-major Division I team that had made it to the NCAA tournament the year before. In fact, a lot of people were saying that Austin Peay maybe had a better team than Vanderbilt, so we knew we were in for another tough test. We played really hard in that game and we played well. Austin Peay had a difficult time the entire game distancing their team from ours, usually holding anywhere from a five to ten-point lead, but we could never quite reach them, and we ended up losing

87-74. After the game everybody in our locker room was disappointed because we all felt that we could have beat them, and when I saw how everybody really believed in our team at that point, I knew that we could have a special year.

Speech for Scholarship Benefit...

After the Tennessee trip, I had to give a speech for the third annual NSU scholarship benefit, and I was really excited to give a great speech. I had been asked months earlier by the committee to be a speaker at the benefit, talking about anything that I wanted to regarding my experiences at Northern. I was hesitant at first to accept the invitation because I had a huge fear of public speaking. In fact, after my freshman year of college I was diagnosed with Social Anxiety Disorder and put on medication to reduce the effects. To say the least, speaking in front of 300 or more people that had followed me as a student and player for five years was a pressure situation that I figured would be a prime candidate for one of my famous panic attacks. Regardless, I was extremely honored to be asked to speak, and I accepted the invitation and began to prepare my speech immediately.

As mentioned above, the speech was the week after our Tennessee trip, so when I was on the road I put on my final touches and figured I was ready to go. I recited my speech in front of my fiancée probably six times in the three days leading up to the speech, and when it was time to give it, I felt as prepared as I could possibly be. The speech was to be given during a lunch benefit, and I walked over to the hall with one of my teammates, Tony Birmingham, who was going to the luncheon as well. While I acted as confidently as possible, I don't think I've ever been more nervous in my life. It's funny how I could easily play basketball in front of 7,000 fans with no worries at all, but when I hopped in front of a microphone, I felt like a terrified child. Walking into the banquet hall I became really nervous when I saw that it was filled to capacity. Luckily Nikki was there when I arrived, and she, like always, did a great job of calming me down and telling me that I would be fine.

To make a long story short, when I actually got in front of the microphone I felt great because I knew the speech so well. I knew that if I could crack a couple of jokes right away to get the audience laughing I would become more comfortable and things would be smooth. Coach Meyer was the butt of basically all my jokes and the crowd loved it, so from the beginning to the end the sailing was actually smooth. I guess the reason I'm including this little story is because walking off of the stage with the crowd cheering loudly was one of the most gratifying moments that I had at Northern. I really felt like I conquered a fear, or at least started to get a grasp of public speaking, and I was proud that I did it.

Starting 5-0...

Finally the games had arrived. The preseason conditioning was over, the grueling "start of the year" practices were over, the exhibition trip was finished, and now it was time to put everything on the table and see where we were as a team. Our schedule that year was particularly brutal and we started off with one of our rivals, North Dakota State, who was a very good team and was moving up to Division I the following year, so we knew it was going to be tough. We felt very confident, however, coming off of our Tennessee swing and playing our first game at home in the Barnett Center. The Barnett Center was always a huge advantage for us because we had amazing fans. Every year we were ranked in the top five in the nation in

151

attendance for the Division II level, and it was very difficult for teams to beat us in the Barnett Center.

Our first game against NDSU was a great game and we clicked from the beginning. NDSU was much more athletic than we were, but we played great team basketball and we pounded them, eventually winning 81-59. We had only beaten two NCC (North Central Conference) teams in the previous four years, so to crush NDSU was a big start to the season. Our second game was also a challenge, but in a different way. We were to play Jamestown College (ND), which was an affiliate of a lower level, the NAIA. However, Jamestown was no ordinary NAIA team, being ranked #1 in the nation. That game was also played in the Barnett Center and we again played great basketball, holding off the Jimmies by a final score of 73-59. As the season progressed, that game turned into a huge win for us because Jamestown didn't lose another game all year, and they beat a lot of the teams in our league. When they went to their conference tournament, I think they were something like 30-1, with the one loss being to us. After the Jamestown game we had three more home games against NAIA teams and we beat them all pretty soundly, moving our record to 5-0 for the first time since I had been at Northern.

SDSU Drubbing...

Going into our showdown with our rival South Dakota State we felt pretty good as a team sitting at 5-0. We knew however that this game was going to be probably the toughest game we played all year with SDSU being ranked in the top ten nationally and having to play the game in Brookings, South Dakota at their gym, Frost Arena. This was going to be our first official road game of the season and we knew that we were physically outclassed, but we still felt that we could pull off the victory if we played well.

Going into the game I had never beaten SDSU since I began my playing days at Northern, so I knew that this was to be my last chance and I couldn't wait to get on the floor. Unfortunately, things didn't quite go as planned and we got absolutely crushed by the Jackrabbits, eventually losing 96-57. It was by far the worst game we had played in a long time, and when the opening tip was thrown in the air we were just plain scared. Our youth and inexperience showed (we started three sophomores, one junior and myself, and two of our main reserves were freshmen), and I felt like I did a particular bad job keeping the team together. I was lost on the floor and I never came close to resembling the leader that a young team in a pressure situation really needed.

A funny thing happened during that game in terms of how the opposing team played me individually. I was never known for my outside shot, and by the time my senior year began Coach Meyer made it clear that there was really no need for me to be taking any three pointers because he felt it wasn't in the best interest of the team. So during our first five games I didn't take a three-pointer and SDSU scouted us well, knowing that I wouldn't be shooting the outside shot. During our game, they played off me at least five to ten feet, and while I was dying to prove them wrong I knew that Coach Meyer wouldn't be happy with my shooting, regardless of whether I made the shots or not. As the game wore on, whoever was guarding me would be sagging all over our post player and we just didn't know what to do. Their game plan worked to perfection, and along with the fact that we were too afraid to compete we were humiliated in front of about 8,000 people.

After the game, Coach Meyer laid into all of us in their locker room calling us scared cowards, and he was absolutely right. No one on the team was above the ripping that night, 153 and Coach let me have it personally, saying that my leadership was nonexistent in a situation where the team needed me the most. The bus ride home was only about two hours but I swear that it felt like ten hours. When we arrived back in Aberdeen, Coach told us to get in the classroom, so at about midnight we had another meeting where Coach Meyer ripped us again and told us it was time to grow up and start playing like a real team.

UND...

After being crushed by SDSU, we had to regroup quickly because we were getting ready to play another NCC power-house, the University of North Dakota. We had a couple of grueling practices, and then it was time to play again. As far as the team atmosphere, I felt that we had regrouped and put the SDSU loss behind us but I also knew that we had to play well from the opening tip against UND to totally regain our confidence. The game was to be played back in the friendly confines of the Barnett Center, and I felt that we would play well.

Going into the game, UND's two leading scorers were both out with injuries, so on paper it looked like we really should have handled them. But as it usually happens, when good players are injured on a team other guys on that team step up, and that was the case with UND. The game was back and forth for the majority of the first half and the beginning of the second half, but after UND hit us with a huge run we never regrouped and as the game winded down, we unraveled again and ended up being beaten by about 30 points (86-54) for the second time in as many games. I had never lost a game by thirty points in my entire career going into my senior season, and at that point we had lost two in a row by that large of a deficit, so confidence for me personally and for the team collectively was really shattered.

The next day during our usual practice time Coach Meyer met with us in our locker room, and for the first time he actually cried. Usually when Coach would become emotional the people around him could see his eyes begin to well up with tears, but nobody that I knew had ever seen him actually cry. So when we met and saw him cry as he talked to us, it was a very emotional deal. Coach Meyer wasn't concerned at that point with X's and O's, but rather he just wanted us to regain the joy of playing. He singled out Dell Mims (our other senior), and I and said that he didn't want our careers to end with memories of games like the ones we had just played. Coach Meyer decided that we weren't even going to practice during the day, but rather he wanted each of us to reflect on what was really important to us, and that was it. As we all walked out of that meeting, there wasn't a single player talking. I think that we were all in shock about what we had just seen. At that point, everybody knew that it was time to get the ball rolling and try to find a way to get moving in the right direction again.

USD...

Our next game was another non-conference battle against another one of our rival schools, the University of South Dakota. We knew as a team that it was going to be tough enough to get our confidence back after consecutive thirty-point losses, and in addition, USD was ranked #3 in the nation at the time so this game was going to be a true test of our character. The game was to be played in the Barnett Center, and even though we had been crushed a couple of times the fans still showed up in droves that night, giving us a great home court advantage.

USD was known for sitting in a zone for the entire game,

155

changing the tempo for teams that only saw a zone defense a couple of times a year. Coach had us really prepared however (we'd practiced their zone break all week long), and when the game started we knew exactly what was going on. I don't remember the numbers from the game, but in the first half we hit so many three-pointers early on that USD stopped playing zone and switched to a man defense, which was very uncharacteristic for them. When they played man defense, it was obvious they weren't comfortable and we took a solid eight or ten-point lead into halftime. In the locker room everybody finally had their confidence again, and we couldn't wait to finish the Coyotes in the second half. There was an air of electricity in our locker room during that halftime interlude and it finally felt like we were playing to win and not playing not to lose the game.

In the second half the Coyotes came out blazing and regained the lead midway through the period, but finally as a team we stuck together when things went wrong. We took the lead back with good team play and as time expired, we had just beaten our highest nationally ranked opponent since I had been a part of the program by a score of 69-57. It was a great feeling being a part of that locker room after the game, not because we had beaten a good team (we expected to beat good teams), but because we had finally come together as a team and overcame a difficult challenge. After losing so badly in the previous two games, to win a game like that was a great feeling. We knew that we couldn't rest on our victory though, because there were plenty more tough games in the road ahead.

Coming Back from Christmas Break...

We had one more game before Christmas break against another NCC team, Augustana College (SD), and we beat them by a score of 78-67, so heading into the break we were sitting at 7-2. Our current record was easily the best record going into the break that I had ever been a part of, so at that point I really felt that we could do something special with the season. While there were always tough conference opponents in the road ahead, many of our toughest opponents from the NCC were already behind us, so things looked good.

At Christmas time, depending on when the players end their class final exams, we were usually able to go home for about four days to spend the holiday with our families and then head back to practice. I remember when we came back and had our first practice after the break Coach Meyer was fired up like I'd never seen him. In talking to him later, his biggest concern at that point in the season was that we would feel content with our record and who we'd beaten in the preseason, and he wanted to make sure that those first couple of practices after the break were as tough as they could possibly be. In retrospect, however, the practices turned really negative and it seemed like the players, including myself, started to lose confidence.

Before we started our regular season contests, we had one more preseason game, a rematch against North Dakota State, who we had beaten by twenty points the first game of the year. This time we were to play them in Fargo, and we knew that they would be ready to go. We came out extremely flat in the game and never mounted any type of positive play, eventually losing 89-71 to a team that we felt we were better than. In the locker room after the game, it was obvious that all the momentum and positive feelings that we left with during Christmas break were gone. That was one of the most disappointing losses of the season and Coach Meyer let us know about it. We had to regroup though, because we were on the road again in two days to start the conference against Moorhead State (MN). We had won the conference regular season title by three games the previous season, so we felt really confident that even with our

157

setback in Fargo, we would be able to get the wheels turning and begin our dominance of the Northern Sun Conference (NSIC) once again.

When we played Moorhead, we played with a lot more energy than in the previous game, but we just played awful basketball. Our shooting was horrendous, we missed a ton of lay-ups and free throws, and we just didn't give ourselves a chance to win. Nevertheless, with only a few minutes remaining in the game one of our sophomore starters, Adam Grant, hit some amazing shots and all of the sudden we were tied, eventually sending the game into overtime. In the extra period we simply fell a little short. We ended up losing to a team that we should have probably beaten by the score of 70-67, and now we were 7-4, 0-1 in conference. Just a few days later, we had to again hit the road and play Bemidji State (MN), who was one of the preseason favorites to win the conference. Bemidji's team was somewhat of a mystery, because many of their guys were junior college transfers, and we had a tough time getting a feel for their style of play and their personnel. They did have undoubtedly the best player in the conference to deal with, a center named Charles Hanks who went on to gain All-American honors, so we knew this was going to be a battle. We again competed hard but just couldn't find a way to get over the hump against Bemidji. With the game coming down to the wire, they hit some huge shots and we missed some of ours, and they beat us 94-83. So now we were 7-5 and 0-2 in the NSIC for the first time in a long time, and we had lost three straight games after the Christmas break.

While Coach Meyer made it clear that it wasn't time to panic, we all knew that if we were going to win our third title in a row, we had to find a way to win some games on the road. I think the thing that frustrated us the most was that we were currently 0-4 on the road for the year. We were approaching January and we still hadn't won a game on the road. Coach always stressed to us that there is no such thing as home court advantage and that it didn't matter where we played ("It's not who you play or where you play but how you play"), so we were frustrated. In fact, during the previous season I think we had a better road record than home record. We knew that if we were going to make any noise in the league as the season continued, we would have to win some road games or we were in major trouble.

"Digging Out Of The Hole"…

As it is said, sometimes great teams must go through adversity before they become great, and we definitely were experiencing our share of adversity. As a team, however, we never lost faith in what we were doing and we continued to work hard in practice to overcome our shortcomings. The following weekend we had two more conference games at home, playing Southwest State (MN) and Wayne State (NE) and we couldn't wait to get back on the floor and try to turn things around. At the start of the conference season every team is usually jumbled in a pack for at least the first four or five games, so we knew that we could climb in the standings, but we also knew that if we lost these upcoming games and started off the league 0-4, we would be in a lot of trouble.

Our first game of the weekend was against Southwest State, one of our league rivals, and we were psyched for the game. I don't think that they could have won that game no matter how well they played because we came out from the opening tip energized and as aggressive as we could possibly be. We entered our locker room with about a ten-point lead and when we came back for the second half, we continued to dictate the tempo of the game. Jared Obering, our junior shooting guard, had a career night with nine three-pointers, and he carried us

159

the whole game. We won the game fairly handily (88-72), and we felt that things were back together. The next night we played Wayne State, who was also one of the preseason conference favorites. Wayne was very disciplined, they had a lot of size, and they played defense. For us to beat Wayne, we knew that we had to play well and carry over the intensity that we had from the night earlier. In our conference, one of the toughest things that a team must do to be successful is win on the second night. When I was at Northern, all conference games were on Friday and Saturday night, so after playing a tough game on Friday, teams had to find a way to recoup and get the victory on Saturday. Playing a tough team like Wayne on Saturday night was going to be a difficult task, but we were ready to continue with the momentum that we had.

The Wayne State game was a very close game throughout, with us maintaining a small lead through the majority of the contest. With about ten minutes left we held about a six-point lead, and at that point our conditioning and defensive pressure took the game over. As Wayne started to maybe fatigue, we continued to press on and we were able to balloon our lead to about twelve or thirteen points, and as time expired we had just won our second league game 80-74, moving our record to 9-5, 2-2 in the NSIC. The Wayne game was a classic example of what happened many times during our games. Usually, our team had a tough time against good teams opening a big lead in the early stages of the game, but as the clock continued in the second half, our conditioning and defensive pressure usually wore teams down. We usually didn't do any full-court pressing or any gimmicks on defense, but for forty minutes we denied all passes in the half-court setting and pressured the ball as tightly as possible, and as games wore on it was plain to see opposing teams start to fatigue. Our defensive pressure and the conditioning that Coach B installed into us won us many games. Coach Meyer always called it "finding ways to win" and for us, playing with extreme intensity on defense was our way of "finding ways to win."

DWU...

The following weekend we played just one game, but it was a big one, playing another one of our conference rivals, the University of Minnesota – Duluth. We played a great game and Adam Grant put on an offensive exhibition, scoring around 30 points, as we defeated the Bulldogs 65-57 in Wachs Arena. Our next game was our last non-conference game of the year against Dakota Wesleyan University. We had won three games in a row and maybe we started to feel our swagger coming back, but whatever it was, we didn't play a great game by any means and we snuck out of our arena with a 70-67 win over an NAIA team that we should have handled very easily. After the game Coach Meyer was very upset because even though we won the game, we really didn't deserve to win it because of how we played. In addition, Coach Sather, our head assistant coach, was even more upset and he let us all have it.

I remember Coach Sather saying, "something drastic has to change," because he felt that we weren't getting the effort that we needed to as a team, and we were all to blame. Both coaches decided that the next day each player was going to pick a half hour slot to meet with the coaches and figure out what the problem with the team was. So the following day Coach Meyer and Coach Sather met with each player individually for a total of seven hours (fourteen guys), trying to figure out what each one of us players needed to do differently to give more to the team. In my meeting, I remember the coaches asking me how my focus was with regards to all the things going on in my life, and I was really upset. But I understood that their questions were legitimate, so I assured them that there was no problem

161

with all of my commitments getting in the way of basketball. In addition, the coaches talked with me about my game on the floor and Coach Meyer made it clear that if we were going to do something special the rest of the season, I had to become the best defender in the conference. Coach had felt that the previous year I should have won the NSIC Defensive Player of the Year award, but it didn't happen. Now, he wanted me to get back into the mode where I could shutdown anybody that I guarded. He stressed that it was vital to our team's success, and I took his words to heart. One other thing did come out of my meeting, and apparently many players voiced the same concerns as I, when it was mentioned that we weren't spending enough time as a team off the floor.

I felt that we should spend more informal time together and a lot of the other guys felt the same way, because we were a team that was fairly evenly divided between real young guys and real old guys, and we all hadn't done enough to bring the team together, regardless of age. As a leader, I felt that I had failed in that regard and I vowed that I would try to do a better job. The next day before practice Coach Meyer met with the team, and the feeling in the locker room after he talked with us was similar to the feeling someone gets after going to confession. We had all aired out our dirty laundry as a team and figured out what the problem was, and at that point we felt that it was time to correct the issue and move on as a team. It was a great idea on the part of the coaching staff to go through with the meetings and see what every single player was feeling at the time. We found the core of the problem and resolved the issue. In retrospect, those meetings with Coach Meyer and Sather and the team meeting afterwards was probably the turning point in our season in terms of us being a team that was barely winning games to a team that finally was united and played as a cohesive unit.

"The Streak"...

At that point in the season, we were 11-5 and 3-2 in the NSIC. We had won four games in a row, and now we felt that things were really coming together. Our next couple of games were again home contests, against Winona State University (MN) who was the preseason favorite to win the league crown, and an up-and-coming Concordia – St. Paul (MN) team. Winona was a team that was much more athletic and much larger than our squad, so we knew that we would have to find ways to beat them fundamentally. The momentum from our mid-week meetings carried over to the game and we played one of our best games of the season. We beat Winona fairly easily (83-71) with a lot of guys contributing throughout the game and truly playing like a team. After the game I felt that everybody had completely "emptied their tank" on the floor, and it was a lot of fun in the locker room enjoying a victory against a good team. The next night we played Concordia St. Paul, and at the half, we were actually losing by a couple points. CSP was playing a zone that we had trouble cracking, but as the second half wore on our depth and conditioning became a huge factor and we were able to get some easy fast break buckets, which ultimately lead to a victory by a score of 76-64. We were currently 13-5 and 5-2 in conference.

The next weekend we were on the road to play Wayne State (NE) and Southwest State (MN) for the second time. Even though we had started to get the winning feeling again, we still hadn't won a road game the entire year (0-4 on the road), so this was to be a huge weekend for us in terms of proving that we could win away from Wachs Arena. We first went down to play Wayne and we knew it was going to be a battle because Wayne St. was one of those teams that was always tough to beat on the road. Also, playing a team for the second time in a matter of weeks is difficult (for both teams) because it's easier to exploit a team's weaknesses and change the game plan. Regardless, we were playing great basketball. We started the game off on a roll, scoring easy buckets and playing great defense and entered the locker room with a about a twelve to fifteen-point lead. The trend continued in the second half and at one point we had nearly a thirty-point lead on a team that was very good in their own gym. We ended up winning 87-73, and we had our first road win of the season.

After the game, we hopped back on the bus and traveled to Marshall, MN to play the Southwest State Mustangs the following evening. As we got into town, something went wrong with our hotel reservations and at about 2:00 am we were scrambling for rooms. We finally found a small motel in town and got settled in around 3:00 am. Our practice was scheduled for 10:00 am the next morning, so there wasn't going to be much sleep that night. After our practice we were able to get back to the hotel and rest for awhile, so all was good. Playing Southwest was always a fun experience for us, because every time we played them, they had their version of "Hawaiian Night," which was also unofficially called "I Hate Northern" night. Their entire student body would dress up in Hawaiian clothes and get ridiculously rowdy during our games. A lot of people asked us if it was tough playing in that type of environment, but as a team we loved to play in a hostile arena because it was intense and it made the team elevate our game. On that night, we played extremely well again and easily handled the Mustangs, winning 70-57. For the weekend as a team we shot almost an unheard of 70% from the field. We were really starting to play great basketball. As we drove back to Aberdeen, we were currently standing at 15-5 and 7-2.

As the season progressed, it was clear that the race for the conference championship was coming down to two teams: Bemidji and us. We were closing in on our showdown with

Bemidji, who had a one-game lead on us, but first we had a road game against the University of Minnesota – Crookston, who was sitting in the last position in the conference, followed by a home game against Moorhead State, who had beaten us earlier in the year. In a very ugly game, we beat Crookston on the road 78-75 and then we handily beat Moorhead 81-66 at home. Our record was now standing at 17-5 and 9-2 in the conference.

Janitor Dan and "Jake at the Lake"...

As the season hits the "stretch run" and gets more intense, it's easy for both players and coaches to lose focus of all the other aspects of life, but Coach Meyer did a really good job of making sure we paid attention to others people's lives, no matter what part of the year it was. Two people that really stuck out in my mind during my senior year were "Janitor Dan" and "Jake at the Lake."

Janitor Dan was one of the janitors at Northern during my days on campus and he had actually been in some trouble with the law and was sent to prison. Knowing Dan on a personal level, it was tough to see somebody that I knew go to jail, but Coach Meyer made sure that everybody on the team still stayed in contact with Dan. As Coach stated, "even though a person is in a bad situation, that doesn't mean that we, as his friends, turn our back on him." Coach Meyer had us set up a schedule where every player on the team wrote Dan letters while he was in jail. We had about fifteen guys on the team, so we created a schedule where each guy had two assigned days each month to write a letter to Dan, and the numbers worked out where he would receive a letter from somebody basically every day. It was a great idea and for the most part we all stayed fairly consistent in writing Dan letters. In return, Dan would write

165

Coach Meyer his own letters from time to time, and Coach would share those letters with us. Every time Dan wrote, it was clear in his letters that just reading whatever we had to say helped him get through the day. To impact somebody's life and help them in a situation like Dan's was a great feeling. Staying in touch with "Janitor Dan" was one of the greatest things we did as a program.

The other person that was a big part of our season was an elderly man nicknamed "Jake at the Lake." Jake was a guy that had been a huge Northern supporter for many years, even sitting courtside the past couple of years. Supposedly, from time to time Jake would even drop by Coach's office to visit and joke around, and it was obvious that Jake held a special place in Coach Meyer's heart. During my senior year Jake had become very ill and was actually forced by the doctor to stay at home pretty much at all times. Not being able to go to our games and the other Northern athletic events was a very difficult thing for Jake to go through, in addition to him becoming very ill. Coach decided that we would go to visit Jake, who lived about ten miles away on Lake Mina, every now and then. We weren't able to see Jake as much as we would have liked to, but when we did make it out to his house it was easy to see the excitement on his face and his wife's face as well. We would hang out at his house for about an hour while he would tell us stories about anything that would cross his mind, and it was a great thing for us to go through and it was really helpful for Jake. After I graduated I wasn't able to keep in touch with Jake, so I never really knew how his condition was resolved, but he touched my heart and taught me a lot in just a short amount of time about enjoying the small things in life. I'm so glad that Coach Meyer was the type of person that felt it was necessary to expose his players to more than just shooting the basketball.

Senior Weekend...

Going into senior weekend, our team was starting to really click. We had won ten consecutive games and we finally had a chance to play Bemidji State again. But, before we got a chance to stake a share of the conference lead, we had to first play Crookston on Friday night. Senior weekend was always a very special weekend. While there wasn't much change for the Friday night games, the Saturday night game was a combination of Parent's Night, the senior's last home game, and the best night of the year for the student body, "I Hate Winter." "I Hate Winter" is basically where the entire student body dresses up in swim trunks and bikinis (keep in mind that the weather in Aberdeen during mid-February is usually about 20-below Fahrenheit), and absolutely get crazy during the game. "I Hate Winter" is to Northern basketball what homecoming is to football. It's a big deal and it's a lot of fun.

My family was able to make it to Aberdeen on Friday along with one of my best friends, Matt Buschy, who had never been to a Northern game before. I was really excited to get the games going and everybody on the team couldn't wait to play Bemidji, but first we had to take care of Crookston. We again played fairly well and beat Crookston going away (85-60), so the table was set for our showdown versus Bemidji. I'll always remember the Crookston game because it was during that game that I finally broke the 500-assist plateau, the second player ever to do so at Northern. Near the end of the game, I had an assist and the announcer roared over the microphone, "Ladies and Gentlemen, Steve Smiley has just moved into second place all-time in assists with that assist, his 500th of his career." The crowd gave me a standing ovation, and I still can't explain the feelings that I felt as I stood on the court as the game was still being played, with all the fans cheering for me. It was an amazing feeling. Even more so, it was unbelievable to experience my 500th assist at a home game and to have my parents Tim & Claudia, my brother Matt, my fiancée Nikki, and my buddy from back home all at the game. I couldn't have scripted the scenario any better than it actually was.

After beating Crookston, everyone was excited but "even-keeled," as Coach used to call it, because we knew that we now had a chance to play Bemidji for a share of the conference lead and we knew that we had to play a phenomenal game to beat them. Bemidji had been playing great basketball all year long and had only one loss up to that point (against Duluth) in conference, so we knew we had to be ready. As far as comparing teams, we were much less athletic than Bemidji and we played a totally different style of basketball. Bemidji loved to run-n-gun and shoot as many three-pointers as they could, while we were more focused on getting the ball inside to our post players and winning with our defense. To be able to play a team like Bemidji with hopes of a conference championship on the line during "I Hate Winter" was a perfect setting. We knew that our crowd was going to be excellent and that adrenaline wouldn't be a problem, so Coach Meyer's biggest challenge for us was to keep us focused on not trying too hard but just to play the same type of basketball that we had been for the past two months.

To say that the Bemidji-Northern game in Aberdeen in February of 2004 was a great game would be an understatement. I would have to say that it was the best game that I ever played in. At the start of the game Bemidji was on fire from three-point land, and they opened a quick lead against us. Probably no more than five or six minutes into the game, with Bemidji holding a narrow margin, Coach Meyer became infuriated when a referee missed a call and he stormed unto the floor, arguing with the referee and earning a technical foul. While Coach Meyer would get mad during games all the time, he very rarely would receive technical fouls, so for him to get one so early in the game I felt that he was probably trying to swing the momentum in our favor. Whether that was indeed his intention or not, it worked. We immediately became energized and as we took the lead a few minutes later, our crowd of about 6,000 erupted. We played well the rest of the first half, hitting big shots and trying to clamp down on Bemidji's shooters and their All-American center, Charles Hanks, and as the clock winded down to signal the end of the first half we were winning by about nine points. Our momentum continued into the second half, and with about ten minutes to go we were up fifteen points and looking pretty good. But, if there was one team in our conference that could erase a deficit that large in a short amount of time, it was Bemidji, and sure enough as our shooting cooled off, they heated up, and with about three minutes left they were suddenly up five points.

Coach Meyer said later that at that point in the game, he wanted to call a timeout but decided not to because he wanted to see how our young team would handle the situation. We could have very easily folded the tent at that point, but instead we remained poised and kept battling. One of our sophomore starters, Matt Hammer, hit some huge shots and suddenly we were ahead by two with under a minute remaining. We had the ball and as the shot clock was winding down, Hammer hit an unbelievable pull-up jumper to give us a four-point cushion and essentially seal the win. When the clock finally read zero, we had beaten Bemidji 97-93 and owned a share of the league lead.

During my time at Northern I would write down notes about everything, because I knew that one day I wanted to write this story. One thing I rarely did, however, was keep track of game stats because they weren't that important to me. After looking at the Bemidji stats, I knew that I would want to include them in the book, because I had never seen anything like the game we had just played. For instance, Bemidji shot

33 more shots than we did, and we shot 34 more free throws than them, which are just astounding numbers in a game as close as ours. In addition, Bemidji made 18 of their 34 three-point attempts, so on three-pointers alone, they scored 54 points and still lost. I had never heard of a team making almost twenty three-pointers, and having their center (Hanks) score 29 points, and lose a game. I don't know who scored all of our points during the game (Hammer finished with a game-high 28 points), but I know that every single guy on our team had to play as hard as possible for us to win the game, and that is exactly what happened. We found a way to win the game, and as Coach Meyer says, that's what great teams do.

As we shook hands with the Bemidji players our coaching staff told us to go back to our bench for a quick announcement, which was a little unusual. Coach Meyer took a microphone and spoke to the fans in the Barnett Center, something that I will never forget. He said that he had waited five years for a moment like this to finally address the fans and thank them wholeheartedly for their support, and it was an amazing scene. Coach started to get emotional and we could hear him tearing up as he spoke. I remember sitting on that bench and just being thankful to be able to experience such an amazing scene. All I could think was that it was a moment like this that made it all worthwhile. I had been in Coach Meyer's program for five years and never seen or expected anything like this, and during my final game in Aberdeen I was able to be a part of Coach's speech to the fans of the Wolves. My only regret was that Sunny (who was in Sweden, playing professionally) wasn't around to be a part of it. I wish he could have been there.

"Humility is the Only Thing that Will Save Us"...

The funny thing after the Bemidji game was that most of the people on campus and around town didn't realize that we still had three more games in the regular season, all of which were road games. I guess everybody just assumed that the regular season was over or something, but either way everybody that we talked to assumed that we had already won the league title. It would have been real easy for us to start believing everyone when they said how good we were, but Coach Meyer knew better. He made sure that we understood that we had a lot of things to work on if we really wanted to do something special in March. He gave us an interesting quote during that week that has stuck with me. He said "humility is the only thing that can save us" and it made a lot of sense. If we started to believe what the papers were saying and what all the people were saying around campus we would have been doomed, because honestly, we weren't that good of a team. We were the type of team that had to come into every game hungry or focused or we didn't stand a chance. Inevitably, Coach Meyer pushed us extremely hard that week to get us ready for a huge road game against Duluth, who was one of the very best teams in the league and a team that always played tough against us.

The Duluth game was a little different than what we were used to because the game was going to be played in the afternoon on Saturday, which meant we had to prepare differently than usual. Our morning practice and meetings were a little earlier than usual, but we were able to adjust and we were ready by the 3:00 pm tip-off. The Duluth game was an extremely difficult game, but it was always fun because they played hard and we had a lot of respect for their squad. I personally enjoyed the challenge because it meant that I had the opportunity to

171

guard the best offensive guard in our league, Sean Seaman. If I was really the best defender in the league, I knew that I had to shut Seaman down and I took it as a personal challenge. The game itself was real rugged and a little sloppy, but we were able to maintain a lead throughout and by the end of the game, Seaman was held to only seven points (on 3-12 shooting). With the outcome still in question, another one of our sophomore starters, our center Aaron Busack nailed a free throw to clinch the victory with a score of 66-62, and we hopped on the bus sitting at 20-5 and 12-2 in the conference with a thirteen-game winning streak and one week left in the regular season.

Final Road Trip of the Season before the Tourney...

Our final two games of the season were against Concordia-St. Paul and Winona State University (MN). At that time we were tied for the conference lead with Bemidji State, so if we won both of our games over the weekend, we would claim our third consecutive league title, and probably hold the #1 seed going into our conference tournament. In addition, we were ranked #4 in the North Central Region (our region was composed of our conference the Northern Sun, the NCC, and the Rocky Mountain Athletic Conference, also known as the RMAC), which was our highest regional ranking since I had been a part of the program. After all the conference tournaments are finished, the regional rankings determine which schools go to the national tournament, and there are a total of eight teams that advance, so the #4 ranking was very important that late in the year. The only way to get into the national tournament without a high ranking was for a team to win their respective conference tournament, which gave the team an automatic bid, so if we didn't win our conference tournament in a couple weeks we had to still be ranked in theory in the top five of the region to gain an invitation.

Since I had been a part of the Northern program, we had never went to the national tournament because each year we had lost in the semifinals of the conference tournament and never had a high regional ranking to get into the national tournament. When the final rankings came out every year, our conference always seemed to lack respect from the powers that be, so we knew that we had to keep winning if we wanted to get a chance to get into the tournament. Of course, if we won the conference tournament in a couple weeks we would automatically be invited, and we had every intention of doing so, but funny things had always happened to us when tournament time rolled around, so we wanted as high of a regional ranking as possible.

With all of that in mind, we left to St. Paul, Minnesota to play Concordia, who was currently eighth in the conference. Concordia was a funny team because even though their record was not good, they definitely were a dangerous team with a lot of talented players. It didn't seem like we were flat going into the game, but there was always a chance that guys were more focused on our game the following night, a showdown with a very good Winona State team, and when the Concordia game tipped off, we most definitely were flat. The first half was really sloppy, and Concordia took a lead on us midway through the half. With time running out in the first half Concordia's best player, Brian Jamros (who I was covering), hit a deep three-pointer and Concordia went into the locker room up nine points. It was obvious from the two team's body languages that Concordia smelt the upset and that we were in a state of shock.

Coach tried to regroup us at halftime, and we started to click in the second half, chipping away at their lead. In fact, near the end of the game we actually took a three point lead, as

173

they had the ball for one last shot. Concordia called a timeout, and in our huddle Coach Meyer made it clear to us that we were going to switch all screens on the perimeter so they couldn't get a good look at a three-pointer. We all knew that Jamros was the guy that was probably going to take the last shot, but they actually had a lot of good three-point shooters on the floor, which forced us to play them honestly. We couldn't afford to leave any of their guys open. As the ball came into play, they started to run some screening action, and Jamros ran off a screen, which we didn't communicate as defenders, and with the clock running out Jamros nailed another clutch three-pointer to send the game into overtime. Concordia was able to keep their momentum going in overtime, and we lost to them 95-87. We went from having a 13-game winning streak, being tied at the top of our conference, and being ranked fourth in the region, to now realizing that the conference championship wasn't going to happen (we all knew that Bemidji wasn't going to drop another game), and knowing that a loss to a team with Concordia's record was going to kill our regional ranking. Either way, we needed to regroup fast because we still had to play Winona State, and we knew that this was a must-win situation.

It was a fairly quiet bus trip from Concordia to Winona that night, as everyone sat back and realized how big of an opportunity we had just blown. Everybody wanted that third straight league championship banner hanging in the rafters of Wachs Arena, and now that wasn't going to happen. The biggest thing that we couldn't do, however, was try to worry about the regional rankings because we had no control over them anyways, so there was no point in worrying about things that we couldn't control. When we arrived in Winona, we set up in our hotel and quickly went to bed. The next morning, we ate at Perkins in the hotel, and it was good to see that everybody was relaxed and in fairly good spirits. I could see that all the guys had put the loss from the night before out of their minds, and now the focus was on beating Winona and going into the conference tournament with some new momentum.

The game against Winona that night was a really strange game. For lack of a better word, the game was similar to a brawl or street fight. Winona came out very physical, and it seemed like their whole game plan was to try and frustrate us through physical play and hard fouls. In a low-scoring first half, we managed to gain a little separation and we went into our locker room at halftime with a small lead. The second half was much of the same in terms of physical play, but as a team we were patient and did a good job of focusing on the game instead of the physical play, and in a must-win situation on the road against a very talented team, we pulled off a 60-47 win. Even though we still finished in second place to end the regular season, everybody was really upbeat in the locker room after the game because we had proven to ourselves that we could win a tough game in a hostile environment when all the chips were on the table. As we drove back to Aberdeen to prepare for the conference tournament, we were currently sitting at 21-6, with a conference record of 13-3. In the previous four seasons that I had been a part of the program, we had never won more than twenty games overall in a season, so when I looked at our record at that point I realized that we could really do something special to end the year. Finally, the conference tournament was upon us.

The Conference Tourney...

First Round

When we found out the pairings for the eight-team conference tournament, we learned that we were going to get a chance to avenge our loss from a week earlier against Concordia-St.

Paul. Everybody on the team was excited to get a chance to play the Golden Bears again, with the chance to redeem ourselves after playing so poorly. We were still ranked #5 in the region at the time, but by then we weren't even concerned about regional rankings and possible scenarios, but instead, all we wanted to do was win our first conference tournament and then get an automatic berth to the national tournament.

The way that the NSIC tournament worked when I was playing was that the top eight teams qualified for the tournament, with the #1 seed playing the #8 seed, the #2 seed playing the #7 seed, and so on. In the first round, the higher seeded (#1, #2, etc.) team had the home court advantage, and the semifinals and championship were both played at a neutral site in St. Paul, Minnesota. We had the #2 seed, so we were to host Concordia-St. Paul in the first round. Going into the tournament, I started to get the feeling that losing to Concordia just a week earlier may have been the best thing that could have happened to us. By not winning the conference title we were really hungry to get the tournament championship, and to lose to a team that we were supposed to easily beat probably made us, as a team, realize that if we didn't come to play every night, anything could happen. Losing probably refocused our attention to "the little things" and made us better in the end.

The first round game against Concordia wasn't even a contest. I wasn't sure how we were going to play going into the game because everybody was really excited to hit the floor, but once the opening tip was upon us, I could tell that it was going to be a great night. We immediately surged out to a big lead and the energy on the floor was amazing. We were hitting shots, playing great defense, and doing all the "dirty work" on the floor, and by the halfway point in the first half we easily had a fifteen-point lead. During a timeout, Coach Meyer let us know that we had to keep the pressure on and not back down. We did keep the pressure on, and by halftime the score was 52-24. The second half was no different, and at one point we were up 70-29. To win in such convincing fashion was a great way to finish my last game ever in Wachs Arena. After the game in the locker room, Coach was talking about different things and then he said something about me that I will never forget. He said, "Steve is, along with Jerry (his son and the all-time leader in college basketball in career assists), the best point guard I have ever coached in terms of running a team, without ever taking a shot" (I had still not taken a three-pointer for the entire season). It was a rare occurrence to hear Coach Meyer give a player a compliment, and in my five years of playing, I had never heard him saying anything like that about me.

After beating Concordia, we found out that our semifinal game was going to be against Winona State, the team that we had just played one week ago. We knew that it was going to be an awfully physical and tough game, and we also knew that beating a good team three times in one year is one of the hardest things to do for a college basketball team. We had about two days of practice and then we hopped on the bus to go to St. Paul, Minnesota to get ready for the semifinals.

Semifinals

The previous two years we had been in a similar situation, easily winning our first round game and coming to St. Paul as the favorite in the semifinal game. We had the #1 seed in the tournament in both of those years, and both times we were beaten by the #4 seed in the semifinals. The funny thing was that a lot of people around town were talking about a "jinx" in St. Paul, where we just couldn't win in that gym for some reason. Coach Meyer made sure that we didn't listen to anybody about a "jinx" and he prepared us for the semifinal game in the same way that we prepared for any other game during the course of the year. There was no reason for us to change anything that we did in terms of preparation; this was just another game and we knew how to prepare, so why change anything?

The game against Winona was played on Saturday night. It was the last of four tournament games played that day (the other men's semifinal and the two women's semifinals), and we couldn't wait to get out on the floor (in an earlier game, UM-Duluth, who had won the tournament the previous two years, shocked the #1 seed, Bemidji St., to advance to the finals). Running onto the floor, it was obvious that we had a huge crowd advantage. It was funny because we had so many fans come to the game that they couldn't all fit into our designated section, so our fans took over about half of the gym seating. Our band and cheer squad also made it to the tournament and as we ran onto the floor, surely enough our band was playing the school fight song. We honestly had so many people there that it felt like a Northern home game. As we went through our warm-up routine before the game I was so excited I couldn't even sit still. Everybody on the team was energized and focused at the same time, and I felt like we had one of our best warm-ups of the year. I could just feel that our luck was going to change this year. So, when the ball was thrown in the air to start the game, I thought we would come out on fire. It didn't happen that way. We came out flat to start the game, not from an energy standpoint, but just from the fact that we couldn't get anything done. Nobody could make a shot and we were turning the ball over like crazy. Winona, on the other hand, was on fire and they quickly took a twelve to fourteen-point lead. We managed to stay in the game, and at halftime we went to our locker room down 32-22.

At halftime, nobody panicked, but everybody was clearly frustrated. Coach Meyer was furious at our performance and made it clear that it was time to decide if we were going to be a real team and "find a way." Going into the second half the coaches decided to make a lineup change, starting our freshmen guard Kyle Schwan instead of our usual shooting guard Jared Obering, who had started every game during the entire year. Luckily "Obi," who had struggled in the first half, was mature enough to stay level-headed and keep his head in the game, because he knew that sooner or later he would have a chance to get back in the game and make an impact for us.

The beginning of the second half wasn't much different than the end of the first half, with Winona hurting us from both the inside and the perimeter, and with our offense struggling to find any balance in our attack. I truly think that we would have been in real trouble except for the fact that Winona decided midway through the second half to change their defense from man-to-man to a zone. Looking back, I still don't know why they changed their defense because we couldn't do anything against it, but for some reason they switched to the zone. At this point, Obi was back in the game, and within the span of about two minutes, we went from trailing 41-28 to having the game almost tied, only because Obi hit four straight three-pointers from NBA range. If Winona wasn't in the zone, there was no way that Obi would have been able to get four looks at a three-pointer, but he saw the opportunity in front of him and he drilled some amazing shots. At this point, our crowd was going crazy and I could just feel the momentum sweeping over to our side.

I do have to give Winona credit because at that point they could have folded, but they didn't. Winona continued to make big plays as well, and for the remainder of the game the score went back and forth between the two teams. I remember making some big plays in transition, finishing a lot of shots in the lane, and I also remember Adam Grant and Matt Hammer hitting some huge shots late in the game. With under a minute to go, the score was tied and we had possession of the ball. Coach called timeout, and we set up a final play to win the game. We decided that we were going to stick with what worked for us, and we set up a play to go inside to our post-man, Aaron Busack. As the play unfolded, we did get the ball inside and Aaron made a good move, but the shot didn't fall, and we were going to overtime. The game was turning out to be a thriller for everybody in the gymnasium.

Overtime wasn't much different than regulation because the score just went back and forth. Adam Grant, who had a tendency to hit huge shots when we needed them the most, hit a big three, and Hammer hit a big pull-up jumper, and with about thirty seconds remaining we had a one-point lead and the ball. As our shot clock was winding down, I had the ball and with nobody open, I drove the lane, finishing a short pull-up near the hoop. Our lead was now three, and Winona couldn't get a good look at a three-pointer at the buzzer. We had finally won a semifinal game (83-80) and advanced to the tournament championship. Our crowd was going insane and everybody was incredibly excited that we had somehow come back from a thirteen-point deficit in the second half to win the game, but we knew that we didn't come to the tournament just to make it to the championship; we had come to win the whole thing and move on to the national tournament.

It was fun to be a part of that locker room after the game. Everybody was in a state of semi-shock that we had won the game, and when the coaches came in, we could see that they were excited. Coach Meyer told us how proud he was that we didn't quit, and we were all so excited for the game the following day. After the game, some local reporters were waiting around the locker room to talk to some of the guys, and one of the reporters that was talking to me asked me how I felt about scoring nineteen points in the game, when my previous *career* high was only fourteen. I had no idea that I had scored that many points, because I never scored in our offense. I told him that I was just happy to help our team find a way to get over the hump, regardless of whether that meant scoring, assisting, or whatever; I didn't care about scoring points, all I cared about was getting that championship.

NSIC Championship

The championship game was to be played at 4 pm on the next day (Sunday). Our semifinal game against Winona, with the overtime and the delays that had mounted during the day, didn't get over until about 11:30 pm Saturday night, so Coach Meyer was obviously concerned about the short amount of turnaround time between games. We went back to the hotel after our Winona game as soon as possible and immediately met in Coach Meyer's room for a quick scouting report. We had played Duluth enough times to know what we had to do, so the scouting report mainly consisted of a quick personnel report. After that, we went to our own rooms and tried to get as much sleep as possible. As always, the key to beating Duluth was to give up no easy baskets and to shut down their perimeter threats, mainly Sean Seaman, their All-Region guard whom I would be guarding throughout the game.

I felt really confident on Sunday morning that we were going to win the game. We had finally "gotten over the hump" and won in the tournament, and we felt that if we played well we should be able to beat Duluth. As we ran out onto the court for warm-ups of the NSIC Championship, the setting was the exact same. Our band was enthusiastically playing the school fight song, our cheer squad was doing what they do, and our great fans were cheering as loud as ever. We had another great warm-up and I felt really good that it was going to be our game to win.

It was obvious that both teams were really nervous. I think that our nerves came from the fact that we had never been to this title game and we were trying too hard. Duluth was probably nervous because they knew with certainty that if they didn't win this game, they weren't going to the national tournament. They weren't ranked regionally, so the hope of an at-large bid was impossible. Early in the game the score went back and forth, with both teams missing shots probably because of nervous tension. As both teams tried to find their footing, Sean Seaman started to take the game over. In a span of about two minutes he nailed two three-pointers and a pull-up in the lane, and I could see that he was planning on a big night. I knew that if he started to gain confidence, he was talented enough to completely take over the game, so I had to try my best to put the clamps on him for the rest of the half and get him out of his rhythm. I was as physical with him as I could be without fouling him, and as the half progressed he missed a couple of shots and lost his rhythm. The other problem that we had to deal with as a team on the defensive end was the fact that Duluth was absolutely punishing us on the boards. There were a couple possessions in the first half where Duluth had three offensive boards in a single possession, and this led to easy baskets. Offensively, we were playing aggressively and getting good looks, but nothing was going in from the perimeter. Aaron Busack did a good job of finishing some shots down low, and I was able to get a couple of easy baskets near the hoop, and we were able to keep the game close. But, late in the first half Duluth made a couple big shots and regained the lead and the momentum, and as the first half ended, they were leading us 30-23.

Luckily, nobody panicked in the locker room. The situation was very similar to that of our semifinal game the night before, and we knew that we could claw back as a team. When the second half started, we tried everything we could to play better defensively and have more of a presence on the boards on both ends of the floor, and we started to make a comeback. Just like the night before, our sophomore forward Matt Hammer made some huge baskets to bring us back, and when it was crunch time Adam Grant scored eight consecutive points, including a three-pointer that was an absolutely amazing shot, and we finally gained control of the game. Duluth hit some three-pointers to keep it close, but as the clock wound down, we were able to hold onto our lead and beat Duluth in a defensive struggle, 63-58.

We had finally won our first conference tournament. As the clock expired, I just remember the excitement that I felt. All of the work that we put in as a team, from the conditioning, pre and postseason individual workouts, all of the lifting, all of the playing, finally came together in that moment. To win the championship as a team, not a group of individuals, made it all worthwhile. We had battled back from big deficits in both of our games, and we had always stuck together as a team. The first person that I found after the clock expired was my fellow senior, Dell Mims. Dell had been through a lot during the year, and he didn't get much playing time, but when I saw him he was just as excited as everybody else. It was a great feeling to be on the floor with that group of guys. We were all going crazy, celebrating, hugging each other, and just letting it out. I remember finding Coach Meyer and giving him a hug. I hugged him and simply said "Thanks, Coach," and I remember him telling me "You're the best, Steve, You're the best."

Once everything calmed down, the tournament committee announced the all-tournament team. First, they announced two players from Duluth, Sean Seaman and Dusty Decker. They followed by calling Aaron Busack's name (our sophomore center), and then they announced Matt Hammer. We were all going crazy, excited to see those guys being honored for their play. There was one spot left, and the committee announced that the final spot, the tournament MVP, was…me. When they announced my name, it didn't really register. I had never been an all-conference selection, and I had never been a guy that was recognized in that sense because I didn't score a lot of points. So when they called my name, it didn't even register. All the

183

guys were going crazy, hugging me and cheering, and then it finally hit me. I walked out to get my plaque, and then we all came together as a team for a huge hug. Looking back, it was probably the single most gratifying moment of my career. Our fans were cheering, the band was playing the school fight song, and we stood at half-court as a team, crowned champions for the first time in the school's history. It was amazing. Of course the ladders came out, and we all cut down the nets. Everybody in our program, from the managers, student assistants, coaches, and players, got a piece of that net. I was the last person to go and Coach Sather, our assistant, told me to just keep the rest of the net. I made sure that I cut a piece off for Coach Meyer, who didn't want to get on the ladder (I think because he wanted the moment to be for his players, not for him), and I made sure I kept an extra piece for Sundance Wicks, who wasn't able to be a part of the moment because he was in Sweden (I felt that if there was any person that deserved a piece of that net, it was Sunny). Things finally calmed down and we went to the locker room to shower up. When we finished our family, friends, and all of the other fans were still on the floor waiting for us. I was finally able to find my fiancée to give her a big hug and to see my mom and dad. I could tell how excited they were and how proud of me they were. It was a great feeling. Right before we left our graduate assistant, Nick Schroeder, came out to tell me that somebody was on the phone looking for me. I knew who it was immediately. Staying up until 3 am in Sodertalje, Sweden was Sundance Wicks, and he wanted to make sure that we got in touch that night so that we could share the moment together. That's why he's the greatest teammate and friend that a guy could have.

Going to the National Tournament...

As we drove back on the bus that evening, we found out whom we would be playing in the first round of the national tournament. The other conference tournaments in our region were wrapping up at the same time and the coaches were on the phone trying to find out what the pairings would be in our regional, the North Central. All of us players were hanging out in the back of the bus when Coach Sather walked back, asking us "if there was one team that we would want to play again, who would it be?" Everybody knew at that point that we were playing the one team that had completely embarrassed us earlier in the year, our rival South Dakota State.

Everybody was excited to play SDSU. We were confident with how we'd been playing, winning 16 of our last 17 games, and we felt that we were a much different team than the scared group that they beat by 40 early in the year. They had been struggling lately, losing early in their conference tournament, and we felt that things would be much different this time around. The other exciting detail of the game and the whole regional was that it was going to be played at the site of the #1 seed, which happened to be Metro State, located in Denver, CO. I was going to be able to finally go home and play in front of my family and friends who had never really had a chance to see me play in the last five years.

The regional tournament was going to happen over our school's spring break, which meant that nobody was going to miss class and we were able to leave for Colorado early in the week to get adjusted to the new setting. The first round games were on Saturday, and we were in Colorado by Thursday morning. We practiced at a Division II school in Golden, Colorado that day, getting used to the altitude and trying to get our legs loose after a twelve-hour bus ride. That night we had a barbeque at my parent's home, with my family and some old friends waiting for us when the bus arrived. We ate like kings, hung out for a while, and then left for the hotel to get some rest. Friday was very similar in that we had a short practice at Metro State in the middle of the day, so there was a lot of down time. Everybody was anxious for the game to start the following day, so time was moving pretty slowly, but soon enough the day was over and it was go-time.

Our game was the last of four games to be played that night. Each regional was composed of eight teams, and the seeding depended on what the game time was. We were the #4 seed in the tournament, and SDSU had the #5 seed, so our game was to be the nightcap. Even though our two teams had probably the furthest travel distances of any of the teams in the tournament, the crowd for our game was far bigger than any other game during the day. I wasn't surprised because not only our fans, but also those of SDSU, were extremely loyal and would travel far distances to see their teams play. Coach Meyer did a good job all week of trying to keep us balanced mentally. This was going to be our first national tournament, so we would undoubtedly be nervous, and the fact that we were playing a team that was definitely a very good team and a heated rival would add to the tension. All week long he stressed to us that we had keep an even-keel, and not let emotion or adrenaline get in the way of what we were trying to do. Coach Meyer believed that if you had to use an artificial high to get motivated, soon enough a corresponding artificial low would follow and things would fall apart. Coach Meyer made sure that we understood that this was just another game and that we were going to do the same things that we always did. He wasn't going to change anything and try to pump us up, and he expected that we go into this game the same way that we went into every other game.

During warm-ups, I could tell that everybody was nervous.

I know that I was nervous. The atmosphere of being in the national tournament was so exciting and the fact that we had the final game of the night in front of a huge, split crowd was indeed a case for nervousness. It seemed to me, though, that we did a good job of using our nervousness to focus on the game and I felt that we had a great warm-up. Everybody was vocal, we were sharp, and I felt that it was going to be a great night. I truly believed that we were going to beat SDSU, avenging our 40-point loss from early in the year, and then move on to the next round. It didn't happen. We were outclassed from the beginning. Although we tried hard, we were physically overpowered and to make matters worse, early in the game, we couldn't make anything. Going into halftime, we were down big, probably by at least twenty points. Going into that locker room, I took a lot of responsibility for the hole that we were in. My assignment was to guard their shooter, Andy Moeller, who was a very good player, but somebody that I felt that I could handle. I was very confident in my defensive abilities, having just been named the NSIC Defensive Player of the Year, and I felt that I could shut him down. For whatever reason, he lit me up. He was hitting deep three-pointers, driving by me for finishes in the lane, and doing basically anything that he wanted. He was a "gamer," the type of guy that could take over a game completely if he was making shots, and on that night he was making his shots. By halftime he already had 22 points, and I felt like I had let the team down. Coach was upset at halftime, because he felt that we could have given a better performance, but he knew that we were trying as hard as we could; it just wasn't happening. He made sure that we understood going into that second half that a true team leaves it all on the floor, regardless of what happens. It's easy for many teams to just "fold up the tent" when they're in a situation like the one we were in, but I'm proud to say that we didn't give up in that second half. We kept trying to chip away at their lead, but nothing happened. SDSU had a much larger team than us and they had more depth than us, so when we tried to exert all of our energy to gain ground, they would simply put in a fresh batch of good players, and we just couldn't catch up. We ended up losing 99-80, and our season, (and my career) was over.

The feeling in the locker room after that game was strange. I was upset because we had lost, but I felt that we gave it our all, and really, there's nothing more that a team can do. I felt like Coach Meyer had prepared us for the opposing team, and I felt that we were ready to go, but it just didn't work it out. Every year when the season ends, our locker room is a strange place. It's rare to find one guy in our locker room that *isn't* crying. Coach Meyer always said that people cry in our locker room not because we lost a game, but because we all knew that we would never have a chance to be on that particular team again. There would be guys graduating and new guys coming in for the next year, so the particular group that just finished the season would never be the same. I always felt like I understood what he was saying when he gave us that speech at the end of each year-ending loss, but I didn't really understand it until I was the guy that would never be a part of the team again. I cried in that locker room with all of my teammates, but I was numb at the same time. I was just finally starting to realize that I would never be able to be a college basketball player again, and more importantly I would never be able to be a part of the family that we had at Northern. I would never have the opportunity to go to battle with my guys in practices and games, and that was the toughest part.

Wrapping it Up...

Once the season was over, everything was different from the time of our last game until graduation. Soon enough, the guys were back in the swing of things with lifting, playing, and individual workouts, and it was an awkward feeling to not be a part of the team anymore. Coach Meyer always made it clear that even when a player finished his eligibility, he was still a part of the Pack, but it was obviously different to not be running around with the guys anymore.

In the spring I tried to find a way to play professional basketball overseas, going to a meat market camp and using whatever contacts that I thought I had to get a contract. It didn't work out, but what I realized was that I don't think I would have even enjoyed it. I loved to play the game and would have loved to play it and actually get paid money to do so, but after my college experience at Northern, I realized that the most enjoyment I had in playing basketball came from being around my teammates. The practices and games were only a small part of what our team was about. At Northern, we did everything as a team. The players lived together, either in the dorms or in "the basketball house," which housed about five or six guys from year to year. If there was a good football game on television, it was a guarantee that everybody on the team would come to the house to lie around and watch the game. If a couple of guys decided to go to a movie, it was pretty much a certainty that every player on the team would get a call. We were like a family, and that's what I miss most about my experience. Even if I was able to continue to play basketball at the professional level, I'm pretty sure that I wouldn't have had the friendships and bonds that we had as a team, and for that reason, I don't think I would have enjoyed the experience. For me, it was never about individual statistics or glory, but about being a part of a group of guys that truly cared for each other and would do anything for each other. I don't miss the game nearly as much as I miss the people and friendships that I built during my short time going to college in little Aberdeen, South

Dakota. I would take a true friendship over a trophy any day of the week.

Coach Meyer...

Obviously Coach Meyer holds a very special part in my heart, or I would have never created this book. It's difficult for me to really describe my relationship with Coach, except to say that I have the utmost respect for him as a person. Most of the people that get a chance to meet Coach Meyer think that he is either weird, or rude, or something that just isn't normal because it's almost impossible to sit with Coach Meyer and hold a good conversation. Coach's mind is always racing a hundred miles an hour, so if a person is talking to him, he may stop in the middle of the conversation to write something down or speak a couple random words into his famous "Dictaphone."

Most people, however, don't get to see Coach Meyer on a daily basis and see how much he cares for the people around him. Every once in awhile, Coach will get real emotional in our locker room and almost tear up as he says that he will do anything for us, the guys on the team. And, when he has a moment like that, everybody in the room knows that he isn't just trying to rally the team or play some type of emotional head game, but instead we all know (or in my case knew) that he is dead serious. Coach would really do anything for us. I truly believe that our program has to be one of the toughest programs in the country to play for, regardless of level or division, because Coach demands so much from us on a daily basis. At Northern, there just aren't many off days. But when it was all said and done and I had just played my last game in the national tournament in Denver, I knew that my experience as a basketball player at Northern would serve me in every area of my life, simply because I was blessed to be around Coach

Meyer and learn his life lessons for five years. He taught me how to completely engross myself in the team concept and worry about other people, instead of putting the emphasis on myself. I will forever be indebted to Coach Meyer for what he taught me, and I thank God that I was able to be around Coach and be a part of his program...

I came back to Aberdeen a few months after I graduated to work summer camps, and I remember Coach Meyer asking me to take a ride with him to put signs up at some local gyms. As we were riding around Aberdeen, we weren't talking about much at all, just talking about random things until we pulled up to the Barnett Center. Coach Meyer had some more errands to run, so he was going to drop me off, and I was leaving the car he stopped me and said "Steve, I want you to know that I love you and let me know if you ever need anything in the future." I was so shocked at the time that Coach actually said that he loved me, I didn't know how to respond. Well, I suppose now is as good a time as ever: Coach, I love you too.

A TRUE TEAM...

After winning the 2004 NSIC Tournament for the first time in school history, we all came together as a team for the group hug (I'm #5). This is probably my favorite picture from all of my days at Northern; this picture defines what our team was all about.

A FEW MORE PICTURES...

From Left to Right:
Top Row: Coach Paul Sather, Tony Birmingham, Student Assistants Jeremy and Devin, Taite Plaas, Matt Hammer, Coach Meyer
Middle Row: Sundance Wicks, Nick Schroeder, Eric Strandberg, Aaron Busack, Dustin Hjelmeland, Steve Smiley
Bottom Row: Student Assistant Adam Nelson, Dell Mims, Adam Grant, Dan Lund, Jarod Obering, Graduate Assistant Ryan Solie

Meeting Coach Wooden: I'm on the left, and my father, Tim, is on the right side. This was taken during the Coaching Academy in the summer of 2002 in Aberdeen, SD. This had to be one of the most memorable experiences of my life.

Coach Meyer giving me instruction during my freshmen year at Northern in the winter of 2000.

Coach Meyer after winning his 800th game against the University of Minnesota-Duluth in the winter of 2004. (Photo courtesy of Nick Kornder, SID at Northern State University – cover photo also courtesy of Nick Kornder)

MEYERISM'S...
SOME OF COACH MEYER'S FAVORITE SAYINGS

(more than a few of these he surely took from other coaches, leaders, etc.)

"You can measure somebody's character by how they treat people that can't do them any good or can't fight back."

"You don't have to win a championship to be a champion."

"A fool despises instruction."

"People don't like you for what they see in you but what you see in them."

"The greatest feelings are expressed in silence."

"You can play with all the intensity of a mad dog in a meat house but if you aren't smart, sooner or later you'll get a bullet between your eyes."

"Start slow, get a rhythm, go fast enough to make a mistake."

"Make practices tougher than games."

"Confidence comes from demonstrated ability."

"Champions don't look at it like a sacrifice;
champions do what needs to be done."

"When the pupil is ready the teacher will appear."

"It's not what you achieve, it's what you become."

"Know who you are and what your game is."

"What you accept in victory, you accept in defeat."

"Do the ordinary things extra ordinarily well."

"Make practices like games and games like practices."

"Happiness begins when selfishness end."

"We have met the enemy and he is us."

"We must practice and play with the intensity
and poise of a national championship team."

"Sometimes a good enemy is better than a good friend."

"It's not what you teach it's what you emphasize."

ABOUT COACH MEYER...

Coach Meyer began his coaching career in 1972 at Hamline University in St. Paul, MN. After three years and a combined record of 37-41, he moved on to NAIA Division 1 David Lipscomb University in Nashville, TN. During 24 years at DLU, Coach Meyer won 665 games and a NAIA National Championship in 1986. He reached 700 victories in only 916 games, becoming the fastest coach to reach the 700-win plateau in the history of college basketball. In 1999, Coach Meyer moved to Aberdeen, SD to become the head coach at Northern State University.

SOME OF COACH MEYER'S ACCOMPLISHMENTS:

- The fastest coach in the history of college basketball to reach the 700-win plateau.
- Winner of the NAIA National Championship at Lipscomb University in 1986.
- During the 1990's, Coach Meyer's teams averaged more than 32 wins per season, more than any other team in the country.
- NAIA National Coach of the Year in 1989 and 1990.
- Assistant Coach for Mike Krzyewski with the Olympic Sports Festival South Team in 1983.
- Coach's teams led the nation in scoring in 1989, 1990, 1992, 1993, and 1995, averaging more than 100 points per game.
- Coach Meyer's system has produced 3 National Players of the Year and 22 All-Americans.
- Coach's 1989-1990 team set the college basketball record for wins in a season with 41.
- Coach Meyer's son, Jerry, played for his father at Lipscomb and broke the college basketball career assist record.
- Two of Coach's former post players, John Pierce and Philip Hutcheson, both scored over 4,000 points in their careers.
- At Northern State, the Wolves have won either the conference regular season title or the conference tournament

in the last four years (regular season in 01-02 and 02-03 and tournament in 03-04 and 04-05).

- Coach Meyer has coached three North Central All-Region players at Northern (Brad Hansen, Sundance Wicks, Matt Hammer).
- Coach's system has produced two NSIC Conference MVP's (Brad Hansen and Matt Hammer) and two NSIC Conference Tournament MVP's (Steve Smiley and Matt Hammer).
- In December of 2005, Coach Meyer won his 800th career game against the University of   Minnesota-Duluth.
- Coach Meyer currently ranks 8th all-time in wins at the four-year level (NCAA Division 1, 2, 3   and NAIA Division 1, 2).
- Over 10,000 coaches have attended the Don Meyer Coaching Academy with featured speakers   such as Pat Summit (University of Tennessee), John Wooden (UCLA), Dick Bennet (Washington   State),   Morgan   Wooten (DeMatha High School), Sherri Coale (Univ. of Oklahoma), Mike   Dunlap (Metro State University) and Herb Sendek (North Carolina State University).
- Coach also produces the 30-tape series "Building a Championship Program" which is one   of the top selling video series of its kind and has been used by Division 1 programs Duke,   Kansas, Wake Forest, and North Carolina and by NBA franchises like the Utah Jazz and Seattle   Supersonics.

For more information on Coach Meyer, and to get information about NSU camps, the Don Meyer Coaching Academy, the "Building a Championship Program" video series, go to www.coachmeyer.com and www.northern.edu.

ABOUT THE AUTHOR

Steve Smiley played at Northern State University from the fall of 1999 through the spring of 2004. Before coming to Northern, he grew up in the suburb of Arvada in Denver, Colorado. At Pomona High School, he played for his father, Tim Smiley. He was the first ever four-year starter at Pomona, a school that had produced two NBA players in the 1970's and 1980's. While his team never made it to the state championship, he did have a very successful high school career. At the end of his playing days at Pomona, he held 13 school records, including being the first ever four-year starter at the school, most points scored in a game (34), most assists in a game (13), and assists for a career (443), among others. Playing in the state's largest classification, 5A, he lead the state in assists during his junior year, he was twice nominated to the all-state team, and after his senior year he was selected honorable mention all-American by three different publications: *McDonald's, Adidas Blue Ribbon*, and *USA Today*. He also enjoyed success in the classroom, maintaining a 4.0 GPA throughout his entire high-school career and being nominated valedictorian of his senior class of greater than 500 students.

Prior to his arrival to the Northern campus, Steve was selected for the prestigious Presidential Scholarship at NSU. After redshirting his freshman year, Steve began his playing days in the fall of 2000. While he was never known as a dominant scorer, he did start for 3 straight years, with his team winning conference championships in his sophomore and junior seasons and winning the conference tournament in his senior year. Steve led the conference in all three of those years in both assist average and assist-to-turnover ratio. Steve finished his career second on the all-time assist charts at Northern (529) and he was only the second player to surpass 500 assists at the university. Steve finished out his senior year by being named the NSIC Defensive Player of the Year, and as the Wolves won their first conference tournament, Steve was named the tournament MVP. In the classroom, he was successful as well, finishing with a 3.85 GPA in the International Business Program. During his time at Northern, Steve would also meet his future wife, Nikki, and the two were married in May of 2004 as this book was being created.

YOU CAN FIND ME
ON THE WEB!

Go to www.SNSbasketball.com for further information on myself, Coach Meyer, and the Wolves tradition, and for information on camps, products, and for free downloads, etc.

Contact Me!

For Information on other books, camp information, or for anything else,
Please email me at
steve@snsbasketball.com.

OTHER PRODUCTS:

The Point Guard Mentality

By

Steve Smiley

Thoroughly details the development of Steve Smiley, team captain, conference assist to turnover ratio leader, and MVP of the conference tournament. Special section on developing point guards by the collegiate record holder for career assists, Jerry Meyer.

The 2002-03 Player Notebook

By

Sundance Wicks

Handouts and notes compiled by Sundance Wicks, four year starter, senior captain, and team leader of the Wolves. Areas covered are mental approach, fundamental checklist, team defense, team offense, special situations and game planning.

Go to www.SNSbasketball.com for more product and purchasing information. To buy additional copies, go to www.trafford.com or contact Steve Smiley at steve@snsbasketball.com for the best price.

ISBN 141207250-6